S.A.I.L.

Self-Awareness In Language Arts

by

Rosemarie Scotti Hughes, Ph.D.
and Pamela C. Kloeppel, Ed.D.

Copyright 1994
Educational Media Corporation®

ISBN 0-932796-63-X
Library of Congress Catalog No. 94-070337
Printing (Last Digit)
9 8 7 6 5 4 3 2

Publisher—

    Educational Media Corporation®
    PO Box 21311
    Minneapolis, MN 55421-0311
    (612) 781-0088

Production editor—

    Don L. Sorenson

Graphic design—

    Earl Sorenson

Rosemarie Scotti Hughes, Ph.D. & Pamela C. Kloeppel, Ed.D.

Table of Contents

Give us your feedback, please!

After you have used all or some of the lessons, please take a few moments to tell us about your use of S.A.I.L.

What did you like best about the lessons?

What would you change to improve the lessons? Indicate specific lessons if possible.

Would you recommend this curriculum to others?

Are there any topics you would like to see addressed in the school through this format?

Please feel free to add additional pages as necessary, because we are very interested in hearing from you.

Please mail or fax to:
Rosemarie Scotti Hughes, Ph.D.
c/o Regent University
School of Counseling and Human Services
1000 Centerville Turnpike
Virginia Beach, VA 23464-5041
FAX (804) 424-7051

Rosemarie Scotti Hughes, Ph.D. & Pamela C. Kloeppel, Ed.D.

How to Use S.A.I.L.

You've opened the manual and you're ready to begin! We hope that you will enjoy using these lessons as much as we have enjoyed designing them.

Each section—Self-Esteem, Decision Making, and Peer Relationships—is preceded by a brief introduction which gives the overall goals of the lessons. Each section has six activities for each grade, kindergarten through fifth grade, a total of 108 lessons. Each lesson is written in the same format: Objectives, Materials, Procedure, Closure, Sailing On (which gives suggestions for alternate and supplemental activities), and Mooring Lines (which lists books, tapes, and poetry relevant to the lesson).

We've included some segments that are generic to all of the lessons. The "Do's" and "Ways to Invite Success in the Classroom" refer to teacher interactions in the classroom. "Turn Ons" and "Turn Offs," verbal, nonverbal, and environmental, are handy reminders for all of us when working with children. "Facilitative Skills" are specific techniques that help children express their thoughts and feelings.

S.A.I.L. may be used in several ways:

- The school counselor can facilitate the first lesson of each section for each grade, and the classroom teacher can then lead the remaining lessons in the language arts/communication class time.
- The school counselor can use the entire curriculum in either classroom guidance or small group activities.
- The classroom teacher may use the entire curriculum within language arts/communication skills lessons.
- The teacher and school counselor may confer, choosing which lessons are relevant for the class, or, which concepts need most reinforcing in small groups and which are most appropriate for the entire class.

Whether you are teacher or school counselor, our intent is to put into your hands a user-friendly curriculum that is relevant to issues facing children today. All of the handouts are copy ready; the materials needed are easily and inexpensively available, and, for the most part, are already in your school.

On the preceding page is a request for feedback. We would like to hear from school counselors and teachers who have used the lessons, because we want to continue producing quality materials to meet your needs.

Thank you for using S.A.I.L. May you have "fair seas and following winds" as you and the children Sail On for the time that your life journeys meet.

Rosemarie Scotti Hughes

Pamela C. Kloeppel

"DO's"

(adapted from the *Teacher-Advisor Handbook,* Norfolk Public Schools, Virginia)

1. DO—maintain a friendly atmosphere by accepting, being courteous and respectful of children's feelings.
2. DO—allow children the right to pass on a response if they feel uncomfortable.
3. DO—listen attentively and actively. Try to really hear what each student is feeling as well as saying to you.
4. DO—keep confidences about your class. If a student says something which raises a concern in your mind, discuss that concern with the counselor, not with other teachers, school personnel, or anyone else.
5. DO—allow children to finish talking without interruption, interpretation, or advice. Do not allow children to interrupt each other, or to make comments while a child is speaking. Equal respect for all must be practiced.
6. DO—accept children's feelings and allow ventilation of strong statements.
7. DO—encourage children to talk to each other instead of to you.
8. DO—remember that your role is to facilitate, to keep the discussion going, but not to do all the talking.
9. DO—keep in touch with the counselor. Refer children, and recommend parent consultation as appropriate, when needed.
10. DO—allow your own humanity to show. Acknowledge that you, too, make mistakes, have problems, and experience feelings just as the children and parents do.
11. DO—show your sense of humor. A smile or laugh from you encourages discussion, trust, acceptance, and group cohesion.

Rosemarie Scotti Hughes, Ph.D. & Pamela C. Kloeppel, Ed.D.

Ways to Invite Success in the Classroom

Adapted from *Fifty Ways to Invite Success in Your Classroom* by William Watson Purkey, Mary Margaret Snyder, and Mark Wasicsko.

1. Arrange a pleasant atmosphere. Displays, bright colors, and posters that are changed regularly brighten the environment. An area rug softens all the hard surfaces in a classroom. Experiment with desk, chair, and table arrangements so that all students feel included.

2. Celebrate. Birthdays are extremely important to children. There are many creative ways to highlight birthdays, too numerous to list here. A special birthday bulletin board, pictures of the birthday children of the month (be sure to include a time for those who were born in the summer months), a special "Birthday Award" from the teacher, a picture or card that each student makes for the birthday child, or a birthday badge to wear for the day are just some ideas to spark your creativity.

3. Treasure Hunt. Have a regular "show and tell" time (even with older students if you re-name it) when you ask: "Among your personal treasures, what is the one thing that you would save in case of fire?" Ask the students to bring the item in and share it with the class. This can be done once a week, until all have had a turn. Then change the topic so students can often be on their feet in front of the class; other topics can include favorite experiences, a good deed done, the best advice ever received, and so forth.

4. Say "no" slowly. Hear each child out. When you are busy, it is better to tell the child you need to think something over rather than say NO immediately. So often, NO is an automatic response. Invite each child to express a request completely before you accept or reject it.

5. Be sensitive with praise. Not all students are comfortable with public praise. Sometimes a private chat letting the child know specifically what has been done well is appropriate.

6. Begin class with a "warm-up." Share a current event, tell a joke you have heard, ask about a popular TV show, or school activity, and so forth before you begin the lesson. Also recognize a child who has earned an honor. It shows that you and they are people first, then teachers and students.

7. Grade positively. Try to focus on what is good on a student's paper; "x's" tell what is wrong. Write positive comments periodically to all students. Also, try to use a color other than red for marking.

8. Share classroom duties. There are many tasks which children are happy to perform, e.g., taking roll, lunch counts, handing out materials, and so forth. You can rotate duties or have an "official

assistant" for the day, complete with badge. Such routine leadership experience builds future leaders. This is not to be someone who is responsible for maintaining discipline or "taking names" if you have to step out of the room. Have a certificate to take home at the end of the day.

9. Share your ideas with other teachers. Set up a "share box" or bulletin board in the teachers' lounge or the office for good ideas in the affective domain; see that teachers are rewarded too.

10. Let the students know that they are missed. When a student is ill, a note or postcard from teacher and/or students tells them they are missed, and they are indeed, an important part of "our" class.

11. Spread positive rumors. Let the class know, with or without mentioning names, something positive that a classmate has done. Remark on small courtesies, the working for improvement, the sharing that you see.

12. Develop class spirit. At the beginning of the school year, encourage the class to choose a "team" name (i.e., a name for their class, not necessarily a name of a sports team), colors, emblem, and motto. These can be displayed in the room and on the door. Mottos can be used on "happy-grams" that students can design, and teachers can copy. They can also be used on messages sent home. These all help develop "team" spirit and involvement as well as pride in and responsibility for the class.

Rosemarie Scotti Hughes, Ph.D. & Pamela C. Kloeppel, Ed.D.

Verbal Turn Ons
Inviting Comments

Good morning!

Thanks very much.

Congratulations!

Let's talk it over.

How can I help you?

Tell me about it.

I appreciate your help.

Happy birthday!

I enjoyed having you here.

I understand.

We missed you.

I'm glad you came by.

What a neat idea.

I care about you.

I think I can.

I want to help.

Welcome!

Merry Christmas!

You're special.

I like what you did.

Get well soon.

I think you can do it.

Please tell me more.

Let's do it together.

I enjoy our time together.

Fine.

You are unique.

I acknowledge that.

That's even better.

I've been thinking about you.

Looking good!

How are things going?

How are you?

I'd like your opinion.

Happy holiday!

I can tell you're pleased.

What do you think?

Let's get together.

What can I do to help?

Of course I have time.

That's OK.

I am impressed!

You make me feel good.

Yes!

Please come in.

I like that suggestion.

I've always got time for you.

May I help you?

Come back soon!

Let's talk.

Keep out!

What Mary is trying to say. . .

Use your head.

It won't work.

You're not trying.

Do not question this policy.

You'll have to call back.

Just a minute.

I don't have time.

This means you.

You can't do that.

I don't care what you do.

Not bad for a girl.

Don't be so stupid!

Sorry, I wasn't listening.

Who do you think you are?

He can't be disturbed.

Why didn't you stay home?

Woman driver.

They don't want to learn.

They don't have the ability.

You can't be that dumb.

They're all in their place.

Who's calling?

You better shape up!

When I was your age. . .

Get off your high horse.

You'll get over it.

I want to have a serious talk with you.

When you're older, you'll laugh about it.

You ought to know better.

You must do as I say.

How could you?

Shape up or ship out.

Anybody can do that.

Why do you bother coming?

That's a childish viewpoint.

Act your age!

That is dead wrong.

Hi, Chubby.

You goofed.

Get lost!

Who's the broad?

I couldn't care less.

That's stupid!

So what?

Because I said so, that's why.

What, you again?

I despise your attitude.

Get out of my way!

Forget it.

You'll never make it.

Sit down and shut up!

I know you're not that stupid.

You shouldn't feel that way.

It's about time.

That's not your idea, is it?

What's your excuse this time?

Nonverbal Turn Ons
Inviting Behaviors

Eye contact	Picking up litter
A relaxed posture	Planting a flower
Leaning forward	Waiting your turn
Loaning a book	Holding a door
Smiling	Tipping a hat
Listening carefully	Extending a hand
Patting a back	Congratulating someone
Shaking a hand	Sharing a poem
Opening a door for someone	Being courteous
Blowing a kiss	Remembering special occasions
A friendly wink	Sharing a sandwich
Sharing laughter	Taking turns
Sharing lunch together	Using a napkin
Being on time	Being honest
Sending a thoughtful note	Offering someone a chair
Bringing a gift	Sharing an experience
Letting others praise you	Giving "wait-time"
Offering refreshments	Sending a valentine
Hugging—when appropriate	Extending an apology

Nonverbal Turn Offs
Uninviting Behaviors

Interrupting

Looking at your watch

Yawning in someone's face

Being late

Scowling and frowning

Slamming a door

Being rude

Using ridicule

Telling a lie

Cutting people short

Making fun of a person

Looking away

Pushiness

Hitting someone

Throwing paper on ground

Gawking at an accident

Using sarcasm

Forgetting a birthday

Playing with your nose

Eating loudly

Showing lack of concern

Having your arms folded

Staring at someone

Littering

Shoving ahead

Stamping your foot

Turning your back on someone

Dumping ashtrays in the street

Insulting a person

Talking with your mouth full

Letting the phone ring

Being obscene

Laughing at other's misfortune

Forgetting a special date

Mimicking

Blowing your car horn

Facilitative Skills

Most of the lessons in this curriculum are based on a combination of teaching and facilitative skills. Facilitative skills are those that encourage children to participate in the sessions. When they are used, they provoke discussion, let a child know that he or she has been heard and understood, lead a child to problem solving, help keep a group on task, stimulate students to take responsibility for what happens in a group, and, in general, enhance the learning environment by showing each child that he or she has value, worth, and dignity.

Teachers and counselors use a combination of these skills. Throughout the lessons, there are opportunities to use facilitative skills. The facilitative skills most often used are listed for a quick review.

Rosemarie Scotti Hughes, Ph.D. & Pamela C. Kloeppel, Ed.D.

1. **Active Listening.** We listen to children all day, but it is our response that assures the child that he or she has been heard and understood. There are three levels of responding:

   a. Reflecting what the child is thinking and feeling about the problem. "You are feeling encouraged because your reading grades are improving." "You are unhappy because you left your lunch money at home."

   b. Responses that demonstrate understanding of the child's problem. Summarize the child's thoughts and feelings by rephrasing what the child has said. "You are feeling discouraged because you want to do better in spelling and you want to find a way to make higher grades." "You are feeling angry because someone is teasing you, and you'd like it to stop." By rephrasing a child's story, you can help the child clarify thoughts and feelings. The child will either confirm or deny your statement; if the statement is not accurate, then you can achieve clarification by asking the child for a summary, or venture another statement.

   c. Responses that help children plan action after you have indicated that you understood their problem. After giving the responses above you can add, "Let's look at some possible ways to solve your problem," or, "What have you tried so far?"

2. **Unconditional Positive Regard.** We must accept children as they are, letting them know that they are O.K., but you do not always have to approve the behavior: "You are a valuable member of our classroom, but when you continually interrupt others it keeps us from learning and we are unhappy." Also, there are generally no "right" or "wrong" answers in S.A.I.L. Asking children how they arrived at their responses will better facilitate discussion rather than looking for the "right" answer.

3. **Feedback and Confrontation.** Giving feedback is commenting on what is, checking whether or not your perceptions and the child's are congruent. "It appears that you enjoy sharing this story about summer vacations" is a form of feedback. Confrontation is noting incongruities, such as, "You tell me that you were happy on the trip, but your face looks sad when you tell about it."

4. **Letting the Group Take Responsibility for its Progress.** Putting questions back to children, such as "What do you think of that?" or "Who would like to comment on what Robin said?" or "We have a problem with some people who do not want to cooperate with the rest of us today," will keep the discussion and the task child-centered. In S.A.I.L. the teacher or counselor is more of a guide than an expert, and the learning and activities are focused on child-centered activity.

5. **Being a Part of the Group.** In S.A.I.L., some sessions ask the teacher or counselor to participate with the children: to self-disclose, to share thoughts and feelings as appropriate, to sit in a circle with the children, to wear similar badges as the children. Participation by the teacher or counselor in group activities allows S.A.I.L. sessions to seem more like a process of discovery than traditional schoolwork.

6. **Use of Questions.** Use open-ended questions rather than those that generate one-word answers or yes/no responses. "Then what happened?" "Describe how you felt." "Tell me more." Open questions facilitate discussion, but closed questions leading to one-word responses shut it down. Also, avoid "Why?" whenever possible, because this can sound judgmental. "What were you thinking (feeling) when you did that" is an alternative to "Why did you do that?"

7. **Please and Thank You.** Modeling or asking politely for children's responses and thanking them for participation and sharing enhance the learning environment when using S.A.I.L.

8. **Inclusion of Non-Participants.** Using facilitative skills generally will encourage all children to participate in the sessions. However, some children require a more direct approach or they may not participate at all. The teacher or counselor can notice which children are not volunteering and make a point of including them. Using a "go-round" periodically, that is, going around the circle or room and asking each child for a comment of some sort includes all, yet does not single out shy children. Asking shy or non-participating children to be an assistant to the teacher or to other children—handing out materials, for example—is another inclusive technique that may eventually lead to comfortable participation. Occasionally ignoring the extroverts and inviting quieter children to lead discussion, by saying, for example, "Charles, whenever you share with us you always have such good things to say; would you like to begin today's session by. . ." is also inclusive.

9. **Body Language.** Seventy-five to ninety percent of communication is non-verbal. Body language that is open encourages participation. Pleasant facial expression, a warm and enthusiastic voice tone, relaxed posture, and inviting hand gestures all convey to children that you welcome the opportunity to be with them in these sessions. They, in turn, are more likely to respond similarly.

10. **The Right to Pass.** Maximum participation by students is desirable. However, at times a child may not wish to share for a number of reasons. Children should always have the option of passing when in a go-round or when called upon. We should always respect a child's right to privacy. If a child consistently passes then you should discuss this with the child; if the child never wants to participate individual counseling may be warranted.

Rosemarie Scotti Hughes, Ph.D. & Pamela C. Kloeppel, Ed.D.

Self-Esteem

Introduction

There is no "typical child." Not one of the children whom you teach fits the description of "average, typical, or normal." Each child is unique—an individual. Each child lives in a specific home environment, has a certain set of genes, and has had separate experiences. Each child whom you teach learns at an individual rate, and is differently motivated to learn. Each child exhibits various behaviors, adaptive or maladaptive, and manifests those behaviors in distinctive patterns. Many outside forces influence learning. Children bring these influences, whether positive or negative, with them into your classroom.

As a classroom teacher or counselor, you are well aware of student differences. You know the same lesson is not received the same way by all students in your class. You also know children will not learn unless motivated to do so. Motivation influences the rate of learning, the retention of information, and the level of performance. Children with poor attitudes about themselves will not be readily motivated to learn.

Strengthening positive attitudes toward self is a first step in helping the student become self-motivated. The motivated student is a successful learner. These lessons help children recognize and value their individuality while appreciating others' differences. Use of the lessons can foster a classroom climate of acceptance and encourage achievement.

Talent Scout

Objectives:

To process auditory information and match it with visual clues

Self-awareness and understanding of how self is seen by others

Materials:

Yellow stars made of paper or felt (optional, see Sailing On).

Procedure:

1. If possible, the children should arrange their chairs (or be sitting on a carpet) in a circle.

2. Explain to the children that today you are going to play a game requiring careful listening and sharp eyes. It is called "Talent Scout." Ask if anyone knows what "talent" means (a definition children might understand is that it is something special, that it is part of you from birth, and involves an ability, like being able to dance, sing, or play ball well, something you can work at to make better). Children also need to understand "scout"—someone who looks for something. They may be able to relate this to the TV program "Star Search," where people with various abilities perform.

3. Tell the children that you are a talent scout today, and that you are looking for talent for your special TV show. There is so much talent in your classroom that you will be describing "talented stars" by giving some clues, one clue at a time. You can say, "If you think that I am describing you, stand up, but do not say anything. When someone stands up, if all of you decide that this is the talented person I am describing, then you all say the person's name together. Does everyone understand?"

4. "Before we begin, let's make sure we can all say each other's names." Go around the circle, beginning with yourself, and have children together say each person's name. You may want to have each child stand when his or her name is said.

Closure:

1. When you have completed the activity, ask everyone to stand and give themselves a round of applause for their talents. Remind them that all are talented, and even though our talents are different, each one of us is special.

2. At the end, thank the children for their participation, letting them know that you enjoyed this special time together.

Rosemarie Scotti Hughes, Ph.D. & Pamela C. Kloeppel, Ed.D.

Sailing On:

Try to include all of the children in this activity. If you cannot, because of time limits, then schedule this in two sessions, morning and afternoon, or two days in a row.

Use only positive or neutral terms to describe the children, such as descriptions of clothing, shoes, hair/eye color, or add a behavior you have noticed that you want to encourage. For example, "I noticed this person sharing crayons with Charles yesterday."

For a quieter ending, you could go around the circle and ask each child to name a personal talent or characteristic.

When the correct "star" stands up, you can ask others in the group to name other talents they have noticed about the person. If you are going to do this, be prepared with something you can fill in with in case no one speaks.

You might want to have some yellow "stars" or paper of felt to give to the children to wear that day.

Mooring Lines:

Barker, Marjorie. *Magical Hands*. Picture Book Studies. 1989.

Nichols, Evangeline. *There's Magic in Me*. Modern Curriculum.

Olen, Jane. *The Emperor and the Kite*. Philomee. 1988.

Happy or Sad

Objectives:

Vocabulary building

Listening skill of attending to a spoken message

Recognition of specific feelings in self and others

Materials:

Popsicle sticks, yellow and blue paper circles, 3 inches in diameter, paste/glue, crayons or markers.

Procedure:

1. Explain that today you are going to play the "Happy/Sad" game, and that they will make the game pieces. Have each child draw a happy face on the yellow circle and a sad face on the blue circle. Paste each circle on a popsicle stick, so that each child has one set, yellow and blue, of happy and sad faces. (An option is to have the game pieces prepared ahead of time.)

2. Ask all the children to give you a big smile, while you hold up the happy face. Invite them to look around at their classmates' smiles. Ask for volunteers to tell about a time when they were happy. Be sure that you also model a big smile and an exaggerated frown when appropriate.

3. Repeat the procedure, asking them to show you a sad, or a "frownie" face. Again, ask for volunteers to tell about a time when they were sad.

4. Ask for additional words that mean "happy" or "sad." You may want to list these in two columns on the board or on chart paper as they are given.

5. Then say to the children, "Now we are ready to play the "Happy/Sad" game. When I say a word that you think means the same as happy, hold up your yellow happy face. When I say a word that means the same as sad, hold up your blue sad face."

   Use the following list, and add others as you choose.

wonderful	terrific	terrible
gorgeous	marvelous	yuk
gloomy	glad	ridiculous
crying	bouncy	snowfall
super	O.K.	nice
alone	hurt	cheerful
down	well	laughing
rain	hot	birthday

Rosemarie Scotti Hughes, Ph.D. & Pamela C. Kloeppel, Ed.D.

Closure:

To end this lesson ask the children to show which words they liked better, happy or sad, by showing either a yellow or blue face. (You could also ask each child to say a word that described how they were feeling today, and to hold up a yellow or blue face as appropriate.) Reinforce the idea that all feelings we have are part of us, and are OK.

Sailing On:

This is a learning experience for the children, so if they seem not to recognize a word, use your facial expression, tone of voice, and body language as clues for them.

Some words are neither happy nor sad, but situational, such as alone—sometimes we may be happy to be alone, but other times we are sad to be alone—so discuss this with the children. In addition, some people may prefer being alone more than others and that's all right, because we all have preferences.

You may use this exercise many times, adding words from stories or activities that arise in class.

You may also want to use this exercise by taking the lead and then inviting the children to add words for the game.

Mooring Lines:

Caseley, Judith. *When Grandpa Came to Stay*. Greenwillow. 1986.

Goodsell, Jane. *Toby's Toe*. William Morrow. 1986.

Liacouros, Aliki. *Feelings*. Greenwillow. 1984.

Sharmat, Marjorie Weinman. *Attila the Angry*. Holiday House. 1985.

Self-Esteem
Kindergarten Session Three

A Feather in Your Cap

Objectives:

Building vocabulary by using words descriptive of others' qualities

To appreciate one's own qualities and talents as contributing to the overall atmosphere of the classroom and the school

Materials:

Newspapers, tape, red paper cut in the shape of large feathers.

Procedure:

1. Have children make newspaper tricorner hats. They may then wear their hats when they sit on their chairs or carpet, in a circle. Explain that hats of this shape were worn by people in the past—as in the story of Robin Hood, for example, and the tricorner hat of colonial times. You might have some pictures to illustrate.

2. Ask the children if they have ever heard the expression, "A Feather in Your Cap." You can explain that in the past, wearing a hat with a feather in it meant that you had received an honor and the feather was the sign to others of that honor.

3. "Today we are going to recognize and honor special qualities we each have." Recall the circle activity "Talent Scout" when we mentioned some qualities that you each had. "Some were qualities we could see and others were talents we knew about you because of how you behave. Other skills you let us know about."

4. "Each of us has qualities and talents that make us an important person to the class. Each of us has qualities and talents that make the school a nicer place for everyone—we each have special contributions to make to our school." You may want to begin by using examples of people the children know, such as "Ms. (or Mr.) _____, our nurse, is very _____ and she or he always_____; or, "Ms. (or Mr.) _____, our principal, is_____, and we sometimes see her (or him) _____. (You fill in the blanks with positive attributes, or, if the children have been in school long enough to be familiar with these people, you may have them do it.)

5. "Each of you has a special quality, and we want everyone to know about it. We are going to take turns telling each person what his or her special quality is today. I am going to write your special quality on this big red feather, and tape it to your hat. You may wear your hats in the classroom and then home today, so that everyone will see how special you are."

6. Have each child stand up in the group, and ask the other children to name a special quality for that child. As each child is given positive comments, write one or two on the feather, and tape it to that child's hat. Put the hat on the child's head. You may want to invite the children to applaud each child as he puts on his feathered cap.

Rosemarie Scotti Hughes, Ph.D. & Pamela C. Kloeppel, Ed.D.

Closure:

End by explaining that it takes many talents to make the world, the school, and the class run well; each of us is important. You might want to conclude by reading *The 500 Hats of Bartholemew Cubbins* or *One Hat, Two Hats*, as an enjoyable, wind-down activity.

Sailing On:

Stress that only positive comments are appropriate for this activity. There will be no put-downs allowed.

Have some comments ready yourself to "help" the group if none are offered for a particular child. You could ask, "What can we say about Kendra's smile?" or, "I am thinking of how beautifully James sings."

You may want to have a variety of colors to use for feathers.

To save time, hats could be pre-made, even at another time as a separate activity.

The hats could remain in the classroom for a few weeks, with the teacher adding words on the feathers as rewards for appropriate behavior, especially those that the teacher would like to reinforce for specific individuals. The entire class could also receive an "extra" feather occasionally for work or behaviors. Be cautious, however, that a contest atmosphere does not develop in collecting feathers—that would defeat the purpose of each child feeling good about self.

Mooring Lines:

A Feather for Her Hair. Modern Curriculum.

Daly, Nicholas. *Not So Fast Songololo*. A Margaret K. McElderry Book. 1986. (Also available in Braille.)

Jossee, Barbara Monnot. *Fourth of July*. Alfred A. Knopf. 1985.

Nidyard, David. *Sometimes I Have To*. Gareth Stephens. 1985. (Also available in Braille.)

Self-Esteem
Kindergarten Session Four
You've Come A Long Way Baby

Objectives:

Application of appropriate conversational skills

Awareness of personal strengths and a sense of accomplishment and growth

Materials:

If possible, a photo of each child as a baby, including the teacher. If baby photos are not available, then use pictures of babies from magazines. For each child, a large sheet of drawing paper, folded in half, and crayons or markers.

Procedure:

1. Ask the children how old they are right now. Hold up a large picture of a baby for all to see and ask how old the baby is. Have a picture ready of a baby that is not yet a year old. Point out that with this baby we are counting in months, because the baby is not yet a year old. Show some other pictures of toddlers, at ages 2 years and 3 years.

2. Next hold up a picture of a newborn, or a baby just a few months old. Ask, "What can this baby do?" The answers should be sleep, eat, wet, mess diapers, giggle, coo, laugh, cry, and so forth. Ask, "Can this baby say the alphabet? Count, Run? Think? Skip? Talk?"

3. Have a group discussion and list on the board (or chart paper) things students can do that they could not do as babies.

4. Hand out the drawing paper. On one half, have the children tape either the baby picture they brought in of themselves, a picture of a baby from a magazine, or a drawing of themselves as babies. On the other half of the paper, have them draw themselves the way that they look now.

5. Put the pictures around the room, and refer to them during the week, reminding the children of the wonderful things that they are able to do because of how much they have grown.

Closure:

Explain that as we grow older, we learn more, and are able to do more and more things. With each day, we can improve. As a closure, or as a follow-up at another time, the story of *Dumbo*, or the book, *Animal Babies*, would be appropriate.

Rosemarie Scotti Hughes, Ph.D. & Pamela C. Kloeppel, Ed.D.

Sailing On:

Children who have been abused may have a very difficult time drawing themselves. Some children abused as infants have no conscious memory of that abuse, but will be unable to draw themselves as infants. If you notice children either having a difficult time drawing, or have produced images that are not appropriate for their level of development (body parts exaggerated or omitted, or drawing themselves as very small, or in crowded corners of the paper) arrange for individual counseling in the school, so that the child can discuss the drawings. Drawings in themselves are only a clue to what may be happening with the child; conclusions should never be drawn on the basis of the drawing alone. It is safer to check out suspicions than to ignore them or draw unwarranted conclusions.

You may want to have a "guess the baby" contest with the pictures before you begin this activity.

If someone in the class has a baby brother or sister, you may want to invite a parent to bring the baby into class.

You can have the same type of discussion as you would with pictures about what children now can do that they could not do as babies.

Another lesson could be about what babies need so they can grow and develop into healthy five and six year old children—love, caring, food, and so forth. You may want to generate a class letter that children could copy and take home to say "Thank you" to those who have cared for them in their lives.

Mooring Lines:

Boynton, Sandra. *Chloe and Maude*. Little, Brown. 1985. (Three separate stories).

Hautzig, Deborah. *Why are You Mean to Me?* Random House. 1986.

Wishing Rainbow

Objectives:

Stating thoughts in complete sentences in front of an audience

Awareness of the importance of individual hopes and dreams and that others may share many of the same hopes and dreams

Materials:

Crayons or markers, a copy of the rainbow handout (page 26) for each child, folded in thirds, with the rainbow on the outside.

Procedure:

1. Ask the children to define "wish." Ask if they have ever wished for anything, and if they did, did the wish come true? Ask the children to volunteer to finish the sentence, "I wish...."

2. "Now think of three wishes that you would like to come true. Your paper is folded into 3 sections. In each section, draw one of your wishes."

3. When the drawing is completed, have the children come to the front of the class, and while showing their pictures, say an "I wish..." sentence for each picture. Emphasize that each child is to speak three complete sentences.

4. When each child has had a turn to recite, have then turn their papers over and color in the rainbow, using a different color for each wish.

Closure:

You could play music while children are drawing, such as "Somewhere Over the Rainbow," "I'm Always Chasing Rainbows," or "Rainbow Connection." As a closing activity, children could learn the words to "Rainbow Connection" (from the *Muppet Movie*). Remind the children that, like a rainbow, people of all different colors come together to make a beautiful world.

Sailing On:

Children may require a reminder about how to be a good listener before the recitations begin. Tell students to listen for wishes that are like theirs. After each child is finished, ask whose wishes are similar to other children's wishes.

You may want to extend the discussion as to wishes that are likely to happen, fantasy wishes or those with a slim chance of happening, such as winning the lottery. You may also want to use this theme as a follow-up lesson.

Rosemarie Scotti Hughes, Ph.D. & Pamela C. Kloeppel, Ed.D.

Children may express some events that seem remote, such as living on the moon. They may give career choices as wishes. It is never too early to begin career awareness, and even living on the moon can be an expressed interest in science. Encourage such thoughts by asking a child what would be necessary to make some of these wishes happen, and specifically what he would have to do in school.

You may want to expand this lesson into two or three sessions, one for the drawing, one for the recitations, and a third for a discussion of similarities and future hopes.

This may be an opportunity to tell the story from the Old Testament of Noah's Ark, always a favorite of children. The rainbow was the promise that the world would never again be destroyed by water. The story has been retold in many children's books.

The rainbow theme lends itself to many activities in the classroom. It can be used as a logo, bulletin board, and can be displayed many ways, such as in mobiles. Children enjoy making rainbows in various forms because of the simplicity of the shape.

Mooring Lines:

Chevlier, Christa. *Spence Isn't Spence Anymore.* Albert Whitman. 1985.

Weiss, Leatie. My *Teacher Sleeps in School.* Frederick Waine. 1984.

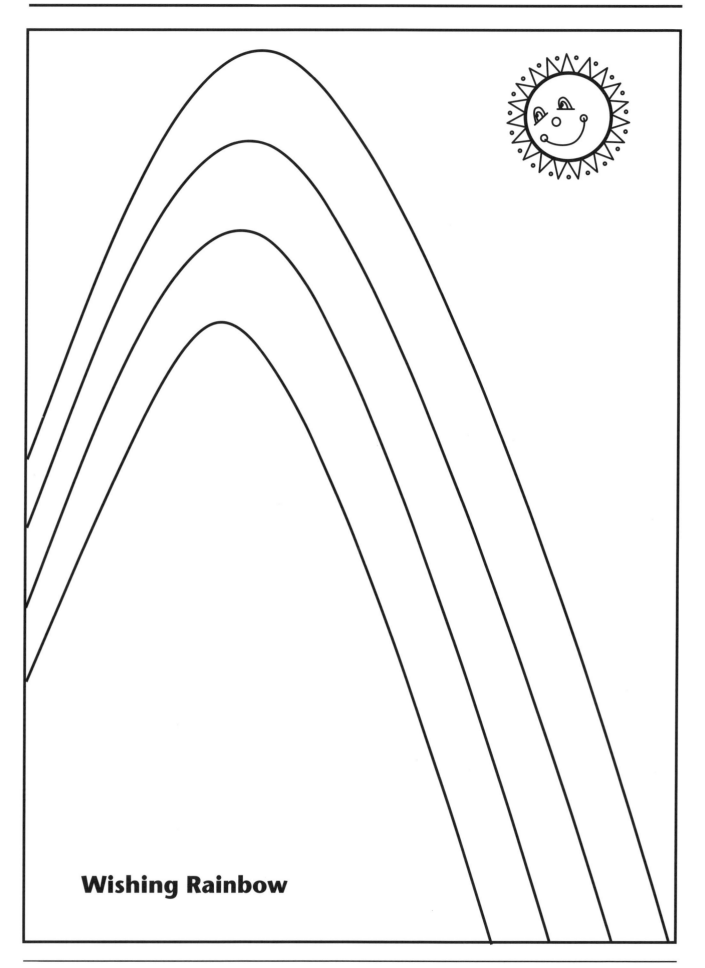

Wishing Rainbow

Rosemarie Scotti Hughes, Ph.D. & Pamela C. Kloeppel, Ed.D.

**Self-Esteem
Kindergarten Session Six**

Snowflakes

Objectives:

Use of descriptive language in writing and speaking

Awareness of similarities and differences among people

Materials:

White paper, scissors, a few pre-made large snowflakes.

Procedure:

1. Hold up the snowflakes and ask the children "How are all snowflakes alike?" (They are white, they have six sides, real snowflakes are cold, they melt, we only see them when it is cold enough, they are pretty, they wet our clothes.)

2. Hold up the snowflakes again and ask, "What is different about snowflakes?" You may have to help the children by encouraging them to look carefully. If you hold up the snowflakes against dark paper it will be easier for them to see the differences in patterns. Emphasize that most snowflakes are different from one another, even though we can't see the differences with our own eyes, we can photograph snowflakes, enlarge these pictures, and then see different patterns. Also, if you live in a climate where it snows, children may be aware of different kinds of snow—"wet" or "dry," good and poor snow for making snowmen and snowballs, flurries that melt when they reach the ground and snow that sticks readily and grows to inches or feet of snowfall.

3. Just as snowflakes have similarities and differences, so do people. Ask, "How are people alike?" You may want to do this in a group discussion,or ask the children to come to the front of the room in 2's and 3's and invite the others to tell what is alike about each group of children.

4. Next ask what is different about people. Explain that no two people are exactly alike, even identical twins, who have different fingerprints and personalities. You can use either method as in #3—either class discussion or asking some children to come to the front of the room, noting differences.

5. When discussions are over, have the children make snowflakes. (You might want to have the paper pre-folded, and assist them with cutting).

6. When the snowflakes are completed (or in a subsequent session), have each child bring his or her snowflake to the front of the room and hold it up and say, "I am like other people because I _____ , but I am different than other people because I _____." Then have the children display their snowflakes, either on the bulletin boards, windows, or other places in the room.

Closure:

"What is the one most important thing you learned from this lesson today?" Have some volunteers wrap up the lesson with their statements.

Sailing On:

Have extra pre-folded snowflakes prepared for children who make mistakes while cutting.

Encourage positive or neutral comments in the children. Do not allow any put-down statements.

You may have to help with the first few statements of differences and similarities. It is important to emphasize that differences are valuable and worthwhile.

At the end of the first discussion of snowflakes, if children have mastered writing skills, you might want to have them copy one or more sentences about snowflakes that were generated during the discussion.

Mooring Lines:

Caple, Kathy. *The Biggest Nose.* Houghton Mifflin. 1985.

Cohen, Miriam. *So What?* Greenwillow. 1980.

Iverson, Genie. *I Want to be Big.* E.P. Dulton. 1979.

Loe, Nancy . *Louanne Pig in the Talent Show.* Carolrhoda. 1985.

Tax, Meredith. *Families.* Atlantic Monthly. 1981.

Wolde, Gunilla. *Betsy & Peter are Different.* Random House. 1979.

Rosemarie Scotti Hughes, Ph.D. & Pamela C. Kloeppel, Ed.D.

Self-Esteem
First Grade Session One
Who's Hiding?

Objectives:

To process auditory information and match it with visual clues

Awareness of how self is seen by others

Materials:

None

Procedure:

1. Children should be seated in their chairs, or on carpet, in a circle.

2. Explain that today you are going to play a guessing game, but before you do, you want to be sure that everyone knows everyone else's name. Go around the circle and have each person say his or her name, beginning with you. Explain that in this game, they will have to use their eyes and be super-observers and pay attention to the people around them.

3. Explain the game, "Who's Hiding?" One person will be asked to leave the room, and then another will be hidden. When the first person returns, that person should be blindfolded and classmates will take turns describing who was hidden, using the phrase, "The hiding person..." rather than with "He" or "She" so as not to give another clue. When the blindfolded person guesses from the clues who was hidden, she or he calls out the name and tells that person to come out of hiding. If the correct person has been named, the hidden person comes out of hiding, and says, "Here I am!" That person then becomes the next to leave the room.

4. Repeat this game several times, as time allows. When everyone has had a turn, ask the children how it feels to be hidden, waiting for someone to guess who you are, and, how it feels to hear other people describing you. Ask if they agree with the descriptions that were given by classmates. Why? Why not?

Closure:

Discuss with the children the clues that they gave—were they mostly about clothing or other things they could see about the hidden person, or were the clues about things they knew about the person, such as the person's favorite activity, or a characteristic, like helpfulness. Include the fact that things we see about a person can change—glasses can become contact lenses; people change clothing, hair cuts or hair color. But what we see about the person is not as important as what is inside.

Sailing On:

You may need the help of a teacher or aide in sending a child outside of the room, to make sure that the child does not wander.

The children may require assistance in speaking in complete sentences.

Have a class discussion of what it feels like to be blindfolded, to guess who was hidden, or to hide waiting to hear their names called.

Another form of discussion can be about which kind of clues were most important in leading to the right answers.

You may want to play this game for 10 or 15 minutes over several days, always leaving about 5 minutes to process at the end.

There are many stories about hiding people and objects in children's literature, particularly in the fairy tales, such as *Rumplestiltskin*.

If you use this activity in the beginning of the year, the children may not be familiar enough with one another to be a successful experience. Therefore, you may want to change the procedure to having the children sit in two circles, with 4 to 6 children on the inside circle and the rest of the children on the outside circle. Or, you could have the smaller group in the front of the room and the other children at their usual seats. Only the children from the inside would be hidden, and, to keep interest, the other children may give clues. When you use this form of the activity, the child who does the guessing will have a smaller number of children from whom to select, and will therefore have a better chance of success.

Mooring Lines:

Cohen, Barbara Nasl. *Molly's Pilgrim*. Lothrop, Lee, & Shepard. 1983.

Hautzig, Deborah. *Why are You so Mean to Me?* Random House. 1986.

Hoban, Russell Conlek. *Dinner at Alberta's*. Thomas Y. Cronwell. 1976.

Marek, Margaret. *Different, Not Dumb*. Franklin Watts. 1985.

Rosemarie Scotti Hughes, Ph.D. & Pamela C. Kloeppel, Ed.D.

**Self-Esteem
First Grade Session Two**

Body Drawing

Objectives:

Listening and attending to others' discussions in a small group

Awareness of one's own physical image and perceptual awareness of body size and space occupied

Materials:

Rolls of brown or white butcher paper, crayons or markers, tape, old magazines, scissors, glue, and a full-length mirror, if available.

Procedure:

1. Explain to the children that today they are going to draw life-sized pictures of themselves, and that they will work in teams of two to do so.
2. Choose one child to demonstrate. Either tape a child-sized piece of paper to the wall or lay it down on the floor, and outline the child in crayon or pencil.
3. After all the children have been outlined, they may then draw in their own faces and clothing on one side only. Encourage them to use the mirror to hold up their drawings and check against their mirror image.
4. Display these around the room or in the hallway.

Closure:

Generate a class discussion on how it feels to have another person outline your body, and how it feels to be the person doing the outlining.

You could also discuss, after drawings are displayed, whether or not these drawings look like themselves. Have children discuss their own drawings so no one critiques art ability of another.

A third closure may be a discussion of one quality each child most likes in himself or herself, emphasizing the uniqueness of each person.

Sailing On:

You may want to allow the children to choose their partners rather than be assigned by you. Keep same-gender children together, even if it means working in 3's.

If you have children with disabilities in your classroom, do not exclude them from this activity. Use an aide or other children who can partner with the child, to include the child with a disability. If there is a physical disability and the child is not able to get out of a wheelchair, discuss some options with the child. For example, there might be another child who matches him or her in height/weight and could be used as a substitute for drawing the outline, and then the child could fill in his or her own unique features; the child could also be drawn in a wheel chair, if he or she wished.

If you notice a discrepancy between what the child has drawn and what the child really looks like, invite the child to the mirror and discuss specifics. For example, "I notice that you are wearing glasses but you did not put them on your drawing. What can you tell me about that?" Stay away from statements such as "You should have..." or "I think you forgot to..." or "This isn't the way you look...." Your goal is to have the child discuss perceptions of self. In the above example, the child may intensely dislike wearing glasses, and wants to appear without them. So do adults, which is why many wear contacts. What is important is that the child's feelings are identified and validated, not accuracy in a drawing.

This activity can be done without taking instructional time. Once demonstrated, assign a place to do this in the classroom, so when other work is completed, students can work on their drawing, or while you are working with one group on another lesson, a separate group can work on this activity, continuing until all children have completed their drawings.

Mooring Lines:

Barrett, John M. *Daniel Discovers Daniel.* Human Sciences. 1980.

Delton, Judy. *I Never Win.* Carolrhoda. 1981.

Drescher, Joan. *Your Family, My Family.* Walker. 1980.

Lexau, Joan M. *I Hate Red Rover.* E.P. Dutton. 1979.

Litchfield, Ada Bassett. *Words in Our Hands.* Albert Whiteman. 1980.

Payne, Sherry Newwirth. *A Contest.* Carolrhoda. 1982.

Stanek, Muriel Novelle. *Growl When You Say R.* Albert Whiteman. 1979.

Self-Esteem
First Grade Session Three

Body Drawing

Objectives:

Same as in lesson two

Materials:

Scissors, tape or glue, old picture magazines.

Procedure:

1. Invite children to look around the room at each other, and then say, "As you look at each other, you can see what is on the outside of each person. You cannot know a person's thoughts, or what things they like to do after school, or their favorite food or TV show. When you drew your bodies, you only showed what was on the outside. Today we are going to talk about what is on the inside of us, and to tell more about ourselves to others."

2. Explain to the children that they are to look for pictures of things that they like, and then to tape them to their body drawings.

3. Invite volunteers to tell about the things that they chose.

Closure:

Have a discussion of what we have learned about each other by showing our "inside selves" on our pictures.

When you feel the drawings have been displayed long enough, help each child carefully roll or fold the drawings to be taken home. Discuss what they might do with these at home.

Sailing On:

You can allow children time to cut out pictures when they have completed other work by having the magazines and scissors available in a separate work place in the room.

Children may enjoy being in small groups for this activity, commenting on each other's choices as they are cutting pictures.

Mooring Lines:

Green, Phyllis. *Gloomy Louie*. Albert Whiteman. 1980.

Hobby, Janice Hale, Rubin, G. & Rubin, D. *Staying Back*. Triad. 1982.

Montgomery, Elizabeth. *"Seeing" in the Dark*. Gerrard. 1979.

Philips, Barbara. *Don't Call Me Fatso*. Raintree. 1980.

Simon, Norma. *Nobody's Perfect, Not Even My Mother*. Albert Whiteman. 1981.

Saying Thank You

Objectives:

Learning social skills: role-playing appropriate language and tone of voice

Teaching appropriate social behavior

Materials:

None

Procedure:

1. Begin by asking what kinds of gifts the children hope to receive on their next birthday. Enlarge the discussion to include gifts other children have received in the past, or would like to receive.

2. Next ask if there are other kinds of gifts. Since the above discussion will probably focus on objects, such as toys, you may have to explain that doing something nice for someone is also a gift, such as offering to wash their parents' car, sending a card to someone who is ill, or writing a letter to someone who is far away.

3. Ask, "When you receive a gift what do you do?" (Response should be to say thank-you). "Yes, saying thank-you is correct, but it is only one way of telling someone that we appreciate a gift." Let's push the ON button in our brains and think of some other words or actions we can use to let others know we appreciate a gift."

4. Begin with a concrete example of someone receiving a gift of a new red jacket for a birthday. "What else could you say besides thank-you?" You could say how much you liked the color, you will enjoy wearing it, it will be nice to have on cold days, it fits just right, you like the shiny buttons, or it has nice deep pockets to carry your stuff. To do this, children may have to close their eyes and first imagine a red jacket, then give you responses.

5. Explain to the children that they are going to work in pairs, with one person being the gift giver, and the other being the gift receiver. Then they are going to do some mini-plays about giving and receiving gifts. Choose the first pair, and ask one what gift would be desired. Then have the giver say, "Happy birthday, Janet, I brought you a _____." Janet will say, "Thank you Jerry, for giving me this _____. I like it because_____ ." Encourage the child to have three things to say about the gift. Conclude with Jerry saying, "You are welcome, Janet. I am glad that_____."

Closure:

Have children discuss whether they liked the role of giver or receiver better; how it feels to make another happy.

You could also conclude by drawing a list of gifts we can "give" in our home and school.

An alternate concluding activity is to choose someone on the school staff to whom the class can write collective or individual thank-you notes.

Sailing On:

Some religions do not celebrate birthdays or Christmas, therefore, you may have to think of another occasion for gift-giving such as when someone graduates from high school, a wedding or Mother's Day.

Some children may need help from you in saying thank-you to the giver for the gift. Give the help when needed, perhaps over-dramatizing to express appropriate emotion.

You may want to have some pictures from catalogs or magazines ready for children who cannot think of gifts themselves. Include pictures of people helping others and explain how this also is a gift.

You may want to do this exercise over several days, about ten or fifteen minutes at a time.

Mooring Lines:

Hughes, Shirley. *Alfie Gives a Hand.* Mulberry. 1983.

Keller, Irene. *The Thingamajig Book of Manners.* Children's. 1981.

Moore, Emily. *Something to Count On.* E.P. Dutton. 1980.

Schotter, Roni. *Efan the Great.* Lothrop, Lee & Shepard. 1986.

Stren, Patti. *There's a Rainbow in My Closet.* Harper & Row. 1979.

Little Fish

Objectives:

Stating thoughts in complete sentences while speaking in turn

Awareness of happy and sad feelings

Materials:

Crayons, copied pictures of fish (page 37).

Procedure:

1. Have the children color one fish red, and one fish blue. Encourage them to add any features to the fish that they wish. Explain that the red fish is a happy fish, and the blue fish is a sad fish. Fold papers so that the red fish is on one side and the blue fish is on another.

2. Have the children sit in chairs (or on a carpet) in a circle.

3. Explain that the class is a school of fish, and that you are a whale who is their friend. "The whale and the fish often play a little game together, and today we are going to play that game."

4. "I will say to you, '(Child's name), little fish, little fish, are you happy or sad?' You decide if you are going to be happy or sad. If you are happy, hold up the red fish, if you are sad, hold up the blue fish. Then I will say, 'Little fish, little fish, WHY are you happy or sad?' and you tell me why." "You might want to tell about something that happened to you that made you feel happy or sad. You might want to discuss something you did."

5. "When you tell me why you are happy or why you are sad, I will ask the other fish, 'Do YOU feel happy or sad about what this little fish is saying?' Hold up either your red fish for happy or blue fish or sad to show us." (You may have to practice this a few times with the children.)

Closure:

Discuss those things the class agrees upon that make them feel happy and sad. Explain that both kinds of feelings are part of everyone's life and that we never have to be afraid to discuss how we feel.

You could conclude with reading *One Fish, Two Fish, Red Fish, Blue Fish*.

Rosemarie Scotti Hughes, Ph.D. & Pamela C. Kloeppel, Ed.D.

Sailing On:

This game gives the children peer support for their feelings.

You can do this exercise over several sessions, ending each with a discussion of feelings similar to and/or different from the "little fish" who is speaking.

The children may want to create a seascape scene on the bulletin board where they put their fish. You might add some happy or sad words for the children to write on their fish.

You could allow the children to choose different colors to express happy or sad, giving out fish from manila paper with "happy" or "sad" written on them; then the children can color in whatever colors they like.

You may want to use other animals in this exercise, such as birds or kittens. A good example would be *The Three Little Pigs*, and the exercise would be "Little Pig."

Mooring Lines:

Delton, Judy. *I Never Won*. Carolrhode. 1981.

Gross, Alan. *What if the Teacher Calls on Me?* Children's. 1980.

Harranth, Wolf. *My Old Grandad*. Oxford. 1984.

Rogers, Fred. *When a Pet Dies*. G.P. Putnam's Sons. 1988.

Thomas, Ianthe. *Willie Blows a Mean Horn*. Harper & Row. 1981.

Waber, Bernard. *You're a Kid with a Big Heart*. Houghton Mifflin. 1980.

Zolotow, Charlotte Shapiro. *If You Listen*. Harper & Row. 1980.

Self-Esteem
First Grade Session Six

Take Charge

Objectives:

Vocabulary building

To help children identify fearful circumstances and cope with feelings of fear

Materials:

Unlined paper and crayons or markers.

Procedure:

1. Discuss times with children when they have felt afraid. Emphasize that everyone has times when they feel afraid, even adults. Tell the children about a time when you felt afraid.

2. Ask the children for some other words that also mean "afraid," or that they think of when they hear the word, "afraid," and list them on the board or chart paper. Some words might be fear, worry, scared, nervous, panic, guns, drugs, emergency, unhappy.

3. Ask the children to close their eyes and think of a time when they were afraid, and then to draw a picture of that time.

4. When drawings are complete, have the children sit in a circle, on chairs or the carpet, with their pictures. Ask them to tell about the incidents depicted. When a child describes the picture, ask if this is something that really did happen or something they are afraid will happen. Introduce the word "imaginary" when appropriate—that sometimes things we worry about will never happen, no matter how much we think that they will. Examples could be bad dreams.

5. Ask the children to share what they do when they are afraid. Explain that sometimes they can do something to change circumstances, e.g., if afraid of the dark, they can ask their parents for a flashlight to take to bed or leave a night light on, if afraid to go to the dentist, think about how the dentist will help them, not hurt them.

6. Ask the children to look at their pictures. Can they change their fears by doing something different, or by thinking something different?

7. You can also discuss how knowing about something makes you less afraid. Ask the students if they were afraid of going to school for the first time; why or why not? Those who say they were afraid (and some may not admit to this, so you will have to use the example of "some other children") were probably afraid of the unknown. Ask the children how they can find out about situations so they will not be afraid—they can ask adults questions, about situations, for example, "What will it be like to go to the dentist? What will the dentist do?"

Closure:

Remind children that they can always find help to deal with their fears.

Demonstrate a technique the children can use when they experience fear, such as deep breathing which puts oxygen into the brain and helps calm them. Practice this with the children, counting to 5 slowly as they breathe in and again as they breathe out. Show how to take air in to expand the diaphragm, and how to release all the air by blowing out.

Sailing On:

When you are disclosing a time you felt afraid, keep it simple, and, related to something the children can understand. You can use an example from your childhood or a common childhood fear, e.g., going down the drain with the bathtub water. Or use a fear from your adult life, such as fear of roller coasters, of a mouse. Don't use a fear that you can't handle, or one that they would not be able to either.

In some homes expressions of feelings are not allowed, especially negative feelings. Refrain from telling children that things will be "all right" or that they don't have anything to fear, because this denies feelings which should be validated. Talking about fears in a group allows children to realize it is OK to feel this way—that everyone does at some time or the other. Also, some fears are very real and will continue to exist, such as fear of violence and crime.

Be alert, in these discussions, for any real situations where children are indicating that they fear being hurt by others. If there are indications of abuse of any kind, the law requires that you call Child Protective Services.

You may want to split this into several sessions, stopping after the children have drawn pictures and proceeding on another day.

You can process the children's pictures in small groups or as a whole class. The important part of this exercise is that you do process the children's fearful drawings.

Mooring Lines:

Hogan, Paula Z. *Sometimes I Get So Mad*. Raintree. 1980.

Hurwitz, Johanna. *Superduper Teddy*. William Morrow. 1980.

Montgomery, Elizabeth Rider. *"Seeing" in the Dark*. Garrard. 1979.

Tanguald, Christine Harder. *Please Help Me, God* (series). Chariot Books, David C. Cook. 1988:

Someone I Loved Died.

Mom and Dad Don't Live Together Anymore.

Guess What! We're Moving.

We Have a New Baby.

Rosemarie Scotti Hughes, Ph.D. & Pamela C. Kloeppel, Ed.D.

Self-Esteem
Second Grade Session One

Bells Are Ringing

Objectives:

Developing skills and manners in using the telephone

Self-confidence in social situations

Materials:

Two real or toy telephones.

Procedure:

1. Have the children sit in a circle on chairs or carpet.

2. If it is early in the year, go around the circle and have each child say his or her name, beginning with yourself.

3. Explain that we are going to play a game today using telephones. Ask, "What do you do when the phone rings? Of course, you answer it! What do you say when you answer the phone?" Let the children give responses. "Today we are going to practice a very adult way to answer the phone."

4. " This is how the game is played: I will say, 'Ring, ring, I am calling someone who...', Then I will tell something about a person, but I will not say the person's name. If you think you are the person I am describing, stand up, and if it is you, I will nod my head, and you walk over to the phone."

5. "When you pick up the phone, this is what you will say: 'Hello, this is _____ speaking; may I help you?'"

6. Make sure that all understand the process, and then go around the circle and have the children practice the answering statement.

7. Next, begin the game. When the child comes to the phone and says the correct response, you say, "I am taking a survey today. Please tell me the name of your favorite storybook." When the child responds, you say, "Thank you very much, _____. Good bye." Wait for the child to say good-bye and you both hang up and repeat the procedure with the next child.

Closure:

Explain that good telephone manners are important so we can share information and be helpful. We want people to be polite and helpful to us when we call them, and in return we show good manners when they call us.

End by asking the children to practice telephone skills by calling each other after school at home. Match children and have them exchange phone numbers. Be sensitive to the fact that some children may not have telephones and be careful not to embarrass any children; keep this part of the exercise strictly voluntary.

Sailing On:

You can allow children time to practice using the phone quietly in a special corner of the room when other work is completed.

You may have an opportunity to add the use of a pay or car phone, how to dial 911 in an emergency, how to deal with obscene or crank calls, how to reach parents who may be at work, or other relatives.

You may want to vary your responses in this exercise by saying something like, "Yes, that's one of our most popular books," or, "That is a favorite of mine also."

Some children may be instructed to use their family's name when answering, as in "_____residence, _____speaking." This seems to be fading out, but be aware that some still do use it.

Many people have answering machines now, and you may want to include a lesson on how to properly leave a message on a machine.

As alternate questions in a survey, you can ask for favorite food, school subjects, songs, colors, or others.

Mooring Lines:

Munsch, Robert. *Love You Forever.* Firefly. 1986.

Roe, Eileen. *All I Am.* Bradbury. 1990.

Golant, Mitch & Bahr, Amy C. *The It's O.K. Series.* RGA. 1986.

    It's O.K. to be Afraid.

    It's O.K. to be Angry.

    It's O.K. to be Different.

    It's O.K. to be Shy.

Rosemarie Scotti Hughes, Ph.D. & Pamela C. Kloeppel, Ed.D.

Self-Esteem
Second Grade Session Two
How Do You Feel? How Do You Say It?

Objectives:

Appropriate non-verbal expression of feelings

Identification of feelings evoked by various words and situations

Materials:

A mirror, if possible; a copy of "Feel it—Say it!" sentences (page 45) for each child.

Procedure:

1. Have the children seated in a circle.

2. Ask them if they know how to show their feelings with their faces only, not using their voices. For example, ask, "Show me how your face looks when you are happy." You can show them how your face looks and tell them you are giving them a BSG (Big Silly Grin).

3. Then, ask the children to identify some other feelings they might know about that they can show on their faces—they will probably first say mad and sad. Introduce them to other words such as disappointed, surprised, tired, proud.

4. Hand out the papers to the children, and read the first sentence together. Ask one child to read the sentence so that all will understand just how that child felt about getting a new kitten. Then ask the children to agree on a specific word which describes how the reader feels about the new kitten. Next, ask the reader to read the sentence again, and show on his or her face this feeling while reading.

5. Repeat the procedure with all sentences. You may use each sentence twice so that all of the children get a chance, depending on the number of children in the class.

6. Next, ask the children to think of something that happened to them that they want to write a sentence about— something that caused a feeling. You can go around the circle and ask each child to state the sentence before writing it. As you go around, you can ask the others to identify the feeling that the person has about the statement.

Closure:

Remind the children that feelings are neither good or bad, they are just feelings. We all have feelings and we need our feelings to be complete human beings. Conclude with each person writing a statement telling a situation which involved feelings.

They could also draw a picture of a situation on the reverse side of the paper.

Sailing On:

Children at this age still have limited vocabularies of feeling words, and so you will have to help them.

It helps children to have their feelings validated, and receive feedback from the other children when they make their statements. Feedback lets people know that they are understood by others.

Some sentences can be interpreted more than one way.

You can use sentences from reading books in this exercise.

You can ask the children if any of the sentences on the sheet actually happened to them, how they felt, what were the circumstances.

Mooring Lines:

Berman, Claire. *What Am I Doing in a Step-family?* Lyle Stuart. 1982.

Buscaglia, Leo. *The Fall of Freddy the Leaf.* Charles B. Slack. 1982.

Hobby, Janice Hale, with Rubin, G. & Rubin, D. *Staying Back*. Triad. 1982.

Moore, Emily. *Something to Count On*. E.P. Dutton. 1980.

Smith, Doris Buchanan. *Last was Lloyd*. Viking. 1981.

Feel It! Say It!

1. I have a new kitten.

2. I lost five dollars.

3. My birthday party had ten guests.

4. I am afraid of the dark.

5. A fifth-grader hit me.

6. Grandma came for a surprise visit.

7. I can't find my new crayons.

8. She called me a name.

9. He is my best friend.

10. I got every spelling word correct.

Now You Write Your Own "Feel It! Say It!" Sentences:

1. _____

_____

_____

2. _____

_____

_____

3. _____

_____

_____

4. _____

_____

_____

Mitten Match-up

Objectives:

To expand vocabulary

To learn and practice the concept of antonyms

Materials:

Mitten Match-Up Sheet (page 48), one per child; colored construction paper, scissors, paste, crayons.

Procedure:

1. Ask, "How many children wear mittens when it is cold? How many do you wear at one time? What are two mittens together called (a pair). Is a pair of mittens alike or different? (alike) Pairs of things do not have to always be the same—for example, a mother and a father are a pair but different." The hot and cold faucets on sinks are different, but together make up a pair of faucets. Those words that go together but are opposite of each other are called antonyms."

2. Feeling words can be antonyms, too. For example, the opposite of happy is ____ (sad). (Some might say mad). Those are word pairs."

3. "I am going to give you a paper with pairs of mittens, but each mitten in the pair is different, because each pair will be a pair of opposites or antonyms."

4. Ask a child to choose a mitten and read the word aloud, then follow the string to the connecting mitten and read it aloud. When the correct pair is identified, have all the children color both mittens the same color. Follow this procedure until all pairs are identified.

Rosemarie Scotti Hughes, Ph.D. & Pamela C. Kloeppel, Ed.D.

Closure:

Explain that the feeling words are in pairs because that is often how things are in real life—we are not always happy, or always angry—we have all kinds of emotions to put balance into our lives. We have many kinds of feelings because we are very complex beings.

Sailing On:

Judge the level of your class and decide if you can have the children do this exercise independently.

Have the children use the pairs of words in sentences orally—"I feel happy when..., but sad when...." and "I feel afraid when..., but brave when...."

The children can cut out the mittens and paste them in pairs on construction paper.

Instead of oral exercises with sentences, use the pairs of mittens in a writing exercise.

You can use words from the vocabulary of your reading series and fill in the blank mitten sheet.

You can also use a sheet of your own design, with pairs of socks, sneakers, slippers, and so forth.

Mooring Lines:

Griffith, Helen. *Alex and the Cat.* Greenwillow. 1982.

Isadora, Rachel. *Willaby.* Macmillan. 1977.

Meddaugh, Susan. *Too Short Fred.* Houghton. 1978.

Waber, Bernard. *You Look Ridiculous, Said the Rhinoceros to the Hippopotamus.* Houghton. 1966.

Weiss, Leatie. *Funny Feet.* Avon. 1978.

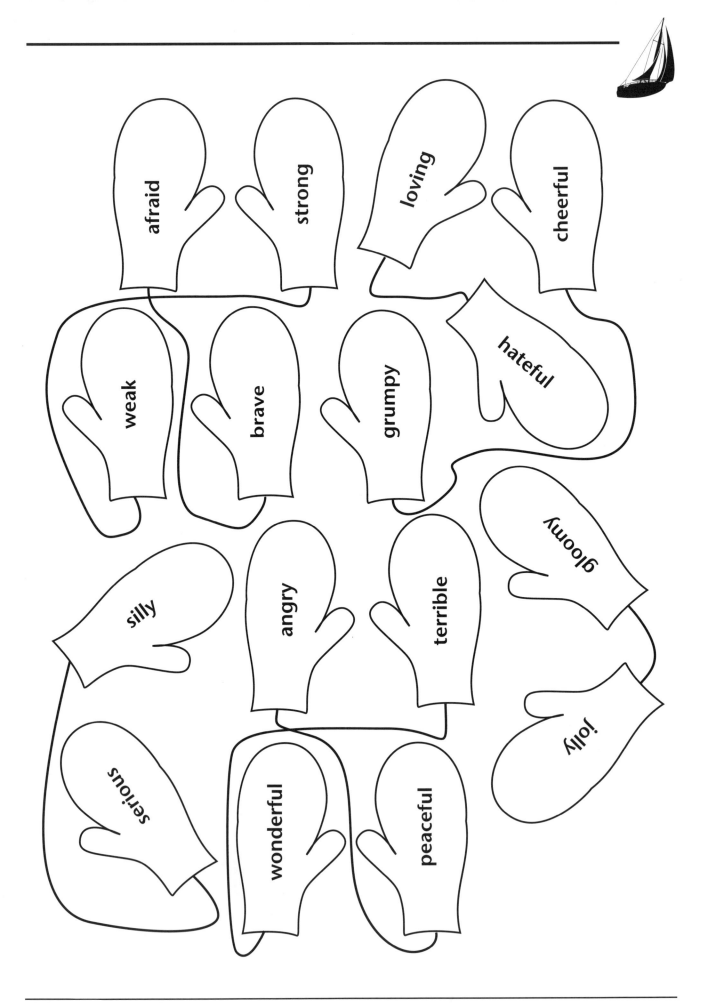

Rosemarie Scotti Hughes, Ph.D. & Pamela C. Kloeppel, Ed.D.

Likes and Dislikes

Objectives:

Formulating sentences about experienced sensations

Declaring individual preferences and affirming individual differences

Materials:

"Likes and Dislikes" worksheet (page 51), one per child.

Procedure:

1. Ask the children to name their five senses. If they do not respond readily, ask, "What does your nose do?" then follow with eyes, tongue, ears, skin, particularly fingertips.

2. Ask for some examples of things that they like to taste, and when they like to taste it. For example, some people like to taste ice cream in the summer, or at a birthday party. Most people do not like to taste medicine when they are sick.

3. Have the children give you some examples of things that they like or don't like and the circumstances. Write the examples on the board.

4. Hand out the sheets and ask the children to fill in the blanks on their own. Help them with spelling as needed.

Closure:

Have the children take turns reading one of their statements to the class. Invite children to raise their hands and tell the class if they have had some of the same feelings which were read. Remind the class that we share likes and dislikes with some people, and not with others, but that it is OK to feel differently from others. It can be interesting to have friends that are different from us, because then we all learn from one another.

Sailing On:

Discussing feelings allows you to get to know your students.

You may want to do this exercise in small groups and do the sentences orally.

Whether you do the exercise orally or written, as a class or small groups, you can allow process time to discuss individual preferences in greater detail.

Mooring Lines:

Barrett, John M. *Daniel Discovers Daniel.* Human Services. 1980.

dePaola, Tomie. *Watch Out for the Feet in Your Chicken Soup.* Prentice. 1974.

Greenfield, Eloise. *She Came Bringing Me that Baby Girl.* Harper & Row. 1974.

Hutchins. Pat. *Happy Birthday, Sam.* Greenwillow. 1979.

Power, Barbara. *I Wish Laura's Mommy was My Mommy.* Harper & Row. 1979.

Rosemarie Scotti Hughes, Ph.D. & Pamela C. Kloeppel, Ed.D.

Likes and Dislikes

1. I like to taste _____

   when _____.

2. I do not like to taste _____

   when _____.

3. I like to see _____

   when _____.

4. I do not like to see _____

   when _____.

5. I like to hear _____

   when _____.

6. I do not like to hear _____

   when _____.

7. I like to touch _____

   when _____.

8. I do not like to touch _____

   when _____.

9. I like to smell _____

   when _____.

10. I do not like to smell _____

    when _____.

Brown Bag Soap Operas

Objectives:

Communication of ideas, concepts, and feelings through creative dramatics

Awareness and expression of individual feelings

Materials:

Brown or white lunch bags, crayons or markers, a puppet of any type for the teacher.

Procedure:

1. Give each child a brown or white lunch bag. Have the children decorate the bag to make a puppet of themselves or any character that they may choose.

2. Have the children bring their completed bag puppets and sit in a circle, on carpet or on chairs.

3. Ask the children if they know what a soap opera or the soaps are; most of them will. For those who may not, explain that they are stories for grownups that are on TV every day. Today, you are going to play "Soap Opera." The rule for this game is that only puppets can talk, so that when students talk they will have to make their puppets talk to the other puppets.

4. Using your own puppet, begin with "Hello, how are you?" to each puppet in the class; encouraging a response if necessary. You could also vary the beginnings with "Hi, what's your name?" or "How are things today?" or any suitable greeting.

5. Use the structured situations on page 54, beginning with "What would you say if...," choosing various puppets for responses.

Closure:

Pair the children and have puppets give a good-bye greeting to each other—such as, "It's been nice talking with you today, Mr. or Ms._____."

Sailing On:

Puppets are an effective way of getting children to respond when they might not otherwise. You might have to remind the children to stay in character as puppets when they are tempted to talk to each other.

You could prepare the class for this exercise by holding a discussion about some characters from favorite stories.

You can have the children make the puppets on one day, and have the exercise on another.

You could do this exercise in small groups or as a class.

In addition to "What would you do if..." you can vary the game by asking "How would you feel if..." to each situation.

Rosemarie Scotti Hughes, Ph.D. & Pamela C. Kloeppel, Ed.D.

Mooring Lines:

Blaine, Marge. *The Terrible Thing that Happened at Our House.* Parents. 1975.

Delton, Judy. *My Mom Hates Me in January.* Whitman. 1977.

Giff, Patricia Reilly. *Next Year I'll Be Special.* Dutton. 1980.

Hutchins, Pat. *Titch.* Macmillan. 1971.

Korschunow, Irina. *Small Fur is Getting Bigger.* Harper & Row. 1990.

Little, Lease Jones. *I Can Do it by Myself.* Harper & Row. 1978.

Ruthstrom, Dorothea. *The Big Kite Contest.* Pantheon. 1980.

Zolotow, Charlotte. *A Father Like That.* Harper & Row. 1971.

Zolotow, Charlotte. *If You Listen.* Harper & Row. 1980.

Brown Bag Soap Opera Situations

1. Your Mom says, "These math papers show me that you have been working very hard at school."

2. Your friend says, "I like to come to your house and play games with you—we have fun together."

3. You are watching a TV show and your older brother or sister comes into the room and changes the channel.

4. You left your lunch at home today and you didn't bring any money to buy lunch.

5. Your pet bird died.

6. You get the chicken pox and have to miss your best friend's birthday/pizza party.

7. Your family is planning a trip to a theme park, and you may invite one of your friends.

8. An older student trips you in the hall at school.

9. The school principal tells you how glad she is that you are part of the school.

10. You tell a new joke to your friends and no one laughs.

11. You want a special toy that you've seen advertised on TV but your parents say it costs too much.

12. You have just learned how to skate on roller blades.

Rosemarie Scotti Hughes, Ph.D. & Pamela C. Kloeppel, Ed.D.

Self-Esteem
Second Grade Session Six

The I-Can Club

Objectives:

Writing a brief personal narrative

Recognition and appreciation of talents and skills in self and others

Materials:

Lined and unlined paper, pencils, crayons, markers, an "I-Can" badge for each child.

Procedure:

1. Ask the children if they understand what it means to belong to a "club." "What do you have to do to belong to a club? When you have met membership requirements, you are a member, and members have some things in common, either something that they are or an interest they have in common, like a stamp collectors club, or a club for people who are identical twins." Some children's concept of a club may be a street gang.

2. "Today you are all going to be in a club. We may all do different things, but we all can do something that is special, and in this class we are going to be members of the 'I CAN' club."

3. Ask the children to think about one thing that they each do well. Invite them to draw a picture of them doing that activity.

4. Next, ask each child to write a short story of a few sentences describing the pictures drawn.

5. Ask the children to each stand and read their stories. When each child finishes reading, have all applaud, and give that child a prepared badge.

Closure:

When each child has read his or her story, hang the picture in a prepared place.

Discuss what a special accomplishment means to us—what can we do with this information, how can it help us in thinking about our future, how does it feel to be recognized by others for a special accomplishment, or to know that you CAN!

Sailing On:

Some children will be more skilled in writing than others; you will have to judge whether or not to write some examples of stories on the board.

You may want to do this activity in two sessions, one to draw, and one to write and read stories.

For some classes, the drawing and oral telling of the stories will be appropriate.

You may want to use the "I CAN" badge as provided, or make something fancier. You may also encourage the children to embellish their own badges at a work center, providing materials and allowing children to work when they have finished other assigned academic work.

Mooring Lines:

Behrens, June. *Fiesta!* Children's. 1978.

Bulla, Clyde R. *Daniel's Duck.* Harper & Row. 1979.

Bunin, Catherine & Bunin, Sherry. *Is that Your Sister? A True Story of Adoption.* NACAC. 1976.

Flack, Marjorie. *Wait for William.* Houghton. 1935.

Harranth, Wolf. *My Old Grandad.* Oxford. 1984.

Steiner, Jorg. *The Bear Who Wanted to be a Bear.* Atheneum. 1977.

_____

is a member of the

"I Can" Club

for special achievement in

_____

Rosemarie Scotti Hughes, Ph.D. & Pamela C. Kloeppel, Ed.D.

Self-Esteem
Third Grade Session One

King and Queen for a Day

Objectives:

Listening to others and speaking in complete sentences

Sharing wishes in a small group

Materials:

Paper crown

Procedure:

1. Ask the children what kings and queens do (rule others, make decisions that other people have to obey).

2. Tell the children that today each one is going to have an opportunity to be a king or queen. Think of some changes that you would like to make in your life. You can change something in our class, our school, your home, your neighborhood or the world.

3. "When I put the crown on your head, you will say, 'I am King _____ or Queen_____ and today I declare that...' and finish the sentence with your wish of what you would like to change.

4. Thank the children for their participation, and tell them that you hope someday they can make their wishes come true. Ask if anyone can think of some things that can be done to make those wishes come true. Discuss the possibilities of making our dreams reality. Has anyone made a wish come true? How? When?

Next Day:

Wishes don't always come true, but sometimes they do. Some of our wishes can be our GOALS in life, and then we have to take responsibility for making them happen. Sometimes we can work toward our goals, even while we are in third grade. We can practice a skill, work at our assignments, and think about how we can be the best that we can be.

Sailing On:

Never criticize a child's statement as impossible. If you are not sure how to respond, simply say, "Thank you, your majesty," and move on to the next child.

Be alert for a child who describes a harmful situation. Alert the proper authorities immediately if you suspect the child may be in a position to be abused.

You might want to ask each child if his or her statement is real-life or pretend. You can discuss whether or not this is a situation the child can do something about, or if it's one of those things that cannot be changed.

Another topic for discussion is what it feels like to want something to change which can't be changed. You might ask the children to write about how they feel in these circumstances.

You can tally on the board each child's statements and determine its category, i.e., home, school, world, neighborhood, and so forth.

However, this might take away from the intimacy of sharing in a group and seem more like a lesson; you will have to determine which is most suitable for your class. You can decide whether to conduct the exercise in small groups, perhaps reading groups, or to do it as a whole class exercise.

You can assign writing a paragraph about the steps to take as king or queen to make the wish come true.

Mooring Lines:

Hill, Elizabeth S. *Evan's Corner.* Holt. 1991.

Hurwitz, Johanna. *Class Clown.* Morrow. 1987.

Lasker, David. *The Boy Who Loved Music.* Viking. 1979.

MacLachlan, Patricia. *Through Grandpa's Eyes.* Harper & Row. 1980.

Schertle, Alice. *In My Treehouse.* Lothrop, Lee & Shepard. 1983.

Steig, William. *Shreik!* DiCapua/Farrar. 1990.

Thomas, Ianthe. *Willie Blows a Mean Horn.* Harper & Row. 1981.

Rosemarie Scotti Hughes, Ph.D. & Pamela C. Kloeppel, Ed.D.

Self-Esteem
Third Grade Session Two

Feeling Faces

Objectives:

Identifying various feelings

Vocabulary building

Materials:

Printed page of blank circles with feeling words written underneath (page 60).

Procedure:

1. Explain that "Today we are going to find out about many types of feelings that we all have. We are going to show those feelings on our faces and then we are going to draw feeling faces. If I asked you to show me a happy feeling on your face, what would your face look like?" (They should all be smiling.) Now, can someone come up to the board and draw a happy face?"

2. Repeat the procedure with "sad."

3. Hand out the papers, and follow the same procedure. For each circle, ask the children to show the emotion on their faces, then draw that emotion in the proper circle. Ask one child to draw the emotion in a circle on the board, and then go on, until all of the circles are completed.

4. Collect all of the papers for the next segment of the lesson.

Closure:

Ask, "How do you feel now that this lesson is over? Show me your feelings on your faces." Discuss the emotions that you see—glad that it's finished, sad because they liked it, tired, and so forth. Explain that you will be doing more work with these feeling faces tomorrow.

Sailing On:

You and your students can create your own "Feeling Faces" paper, using vocabulary words from reading lessons.

Mooring Lines:

Brandenberg, Franz. *I Wish I was Sick, Too!* Greenwillow. 1976.

Farger, Norma. *How Does it Feel to be Old?* Dutton Children's. 1979.

Fleischman, Paul. *The Animal Hedge.* Dutton Children's. 1983.

Lasker, Joe. *Nick Joins In.* Whitman. 1980.

MacLachlan, Pat. *Mama One, Mama Two.* Harper & Row. 1982.

Stanek, Muriel. *Don't Hurt Me, Mama.* Whitman. 1983.

Yashima, Taro. *Crow Boy.* Viking. 1955.

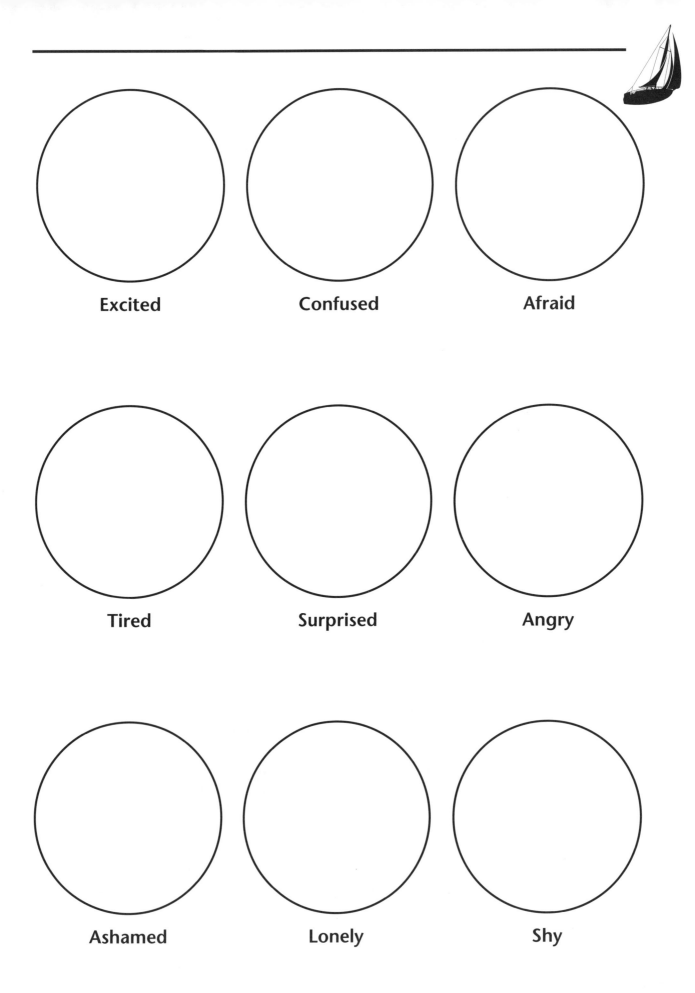

Excited

Confused

Afraid

Tired

Surprised

Angry

Ashamed

Lonely

Shy

Rosemarie Scotti Hughes, Ph.D. & Pamela C. Kloeppel, Ed.D.

Self-Esteem
Third Grade Session Three

Color Me Terrific

Objectives:

Assist children in understanding emotions

Oral expression of emotions

Materials:

Feeling faces sheets from previous session, crayons.

Procedure:

1. Ask the children if they know what it means to feel "blue, tickled-pink, green with envy, or red-hot." Ask the children to give examples of times when they or others have felt this way. Did the person's skin really change color? Did they change color on the inside? In their brain? Of course not!! But we do speak of feelings in terms of colors.

2. Ask some children to tell their favorite colors. Do they know why the color is their favorite? Do they have a feeling about the color?

3. Hand out the Feeling Faces sheets from the previous session. Review each feeling one by one, and ask the children to color in each face as it is reviewed with a color they associate with that feeling. In your review, you might ask someone to use the word in a sentence, or to write the sentence on the board.

4. When the children have completed coloring, ask them to share some times when they have experienced these feelings. Write on the board, "I felt _____when _____. I chose the color_____ for this feeling because_____." When the child has finished sharing, ask for another statement about the same feeling. Compare and contrast how different students see the same emotion as being a different color.

Closure:

"When we discuss how we feel, we do not talk about what are correct or incorrect feelings; we talk about what an emotion means to us personally. We often see things differently; thank you for being willing to share how you feel."

Sailing On:

Be alert for any situations that might warrant individual counseling. Any suspicions of physical or sexual abuse of the child must, by law, be reported to Child Protective Services.

Mooring Lines:

Anderson, Hans Christian. *The Ugly Duckling*. Harcourt. 1979.

Baylor, Byrd. *The Best Town in the World*. Scribner's. 1983.

Blume, Judy. *Freckle Juice*. Four Winds. 1971.

Carle, Eric. *The Mixed-up Chameleon*. Harper & Row. 1984.

Conlin, Susan & Levine-Friedman, Susan. *Lets Talk About Feelings: Ellie's Day*. Parenting. 1989.

Demi. *Liang and the Magic Paintbrush*. Fitzhenry & Whiteside. 1980.

Howe, James. *I Wish I Were a Butterfly*. Harcourt. 1987.

Lionni, Leo. *Color of His Own*. Pantheon. 1975.

Palmer, Pat. *Liking Myself*. Impact. 1977.

Preston, Edna Mitchell. *The Temper Tantrum Book*. Puffin. 1976.

Shles, Larry. *Moths & Mothers/ Feathers & Fathers*.

Singer, Marilyn. *Turtle in July*. Macmillan. 1989.

Steig, William. *Brave Irene*. Sunburst. 1986.

White, E.B. *Charlotte's Web*. HarperCollins. 1952.

Yashima, Taro. *Crow Boy*. Viking. 1955.

Rosemarie Scotti Hughes, Ph.D. & Pamela C. Kloeppel, Ed.D.

Self-Esteem
Third Grade Session Four

I am Hand-y

Objectives:

Awareness of benefits of being a helper to others
Vocabulary development

Materials:

White or light-colored construction paper, pencils, crayons/markers.

Procedure:

1. Ask the children what kinds of things we do with our hands in the following situations (list them on the board so you can write in columns underneath)—things we do for ourselves, things we do to help others, things we do that hurt others.

2. Ask the children to describe how they feel when they use their hands for themselves (e.g., learn to play an instrument, to catch a ball, to make a craft item, to improve their appearance, and so forth). Next ask about feelings in the other two categories—which gives us good feelings about ourselves, helping others or hurting others. Help children understand that people are grateful when they are helped, and other's gratitude makes us feel good about ourselves.

3. Pass out the art materials if you have not already done so, and demonstrate to children how they are to trace their hands, side by side, on the paper. Next, the children are to write on the thumbs and fingers things that they do to help others. They can decorate the hands, and/or cut them out. The hands can be displayed around the room.

Closure:

Have the children shake hands with each other and say to one another, "Congratulations on being a helper."

Sailing On:

Some children may state that they would feel good by hurting another, to retaliate for a wrong done by another. If this does occur, discuss how no one wins in that kind of a situation. There may be times when you have to defend yourself, when you may hit another back so he will leave you alone in the future. Such a situation creates good feelings only because you have taken care of yourself. But when you hurt another just to hurt, you do not feel good about yourself at all, in fact, it will just make you feel worse.

Mooring Lines:

Andrews, Jan. *Very Last First Time.* McElderly. *1986.*

Byars, Betsy. *Not-Just-Anybody Family.* Delacorte. 1986.

Forte, Imogene. *From A to Z With Me: A Self-Concept Activity Book for Young Children.* Incentive. 1981.

Gaitskill, Susan. *Emily.* Three Trees Press. 1986.

Kraus, Robert. *Herman the Helper.* Prentice-Hall. 1987.

Kraus, Robert. *Leo, the Late Bloomer.* Windmill. 1987.

Krauss, Ruth & Johnson, Crockett. *Is This You?* Scholastic. 1955.

Marton, Jinina. *I'll do it Myself.* Firefly. 1989.

Roop, Connie & Roop, Peter. *Keep the Lights Burning, Abbie.* Carolrhoda. 1985. (Also available in video, 30 mi., Reading Rainbow Series.)

Ross, Dave. *A Book of Hugs.* HarperCollins. 1980.

Schwartz, Linda. *I am Special.* Learning Works. 1978.

Silverstein, Shel. *The Giving Tree.* HarperCollins. 1964.

Steig, William. *Brave Irene.* Sunburst. 1986.

VanLaan, Nancy. *Rainbow Crow.* Random House. 1989.

Zilger, Linda (ed.). *Let's Grow: Seventy-two Gardening Adventures with Children.* Garden Way. 1988.

Rosemarie Scotti Hughes, Ph.D. & Pamela C. Kloeppel, Ed.D.

Self-Esteem
Third Grade Session Five

Happy Birthday

Objectives:

Communicating wishes and desires to others

Descriptive writing

Materials:

Plain paper, lined paper, crayons/markers, pencils, empty boxes wrapped as gifts.

Procedure:

1. Display the wrapped boxes to the children. (It would be nice if you could have several sizes and shapes.) Tell the children to pretend that today is everyone's birthday, and that in one of these boxes is their "ideal" present, the one thing that they want more than anything else. Explain that their present might require a box of a different shape or size, but they can pretend that they are magic boxes, able to hold whatever they want.

2. Ask the children to draw a picture of what this wonderful present would be.

3. Next, write on the board, "I would like to receive a _____ for my birthday. It is _____..." Have children write descriptive paragraphs about this gift, beginning with this sentence.

4. Have children read their stories aloud. Display stories and pictures in the room.

Closure:

When you complete this activity, have all the children sing "Happy Birthday to Us." Wish them a happy day and tell them that you hope that all of their dreams come true.

Sailing On:

Some religions do not celebrate birthdays. If you have a child for whom this would be inappropriate, you can have the child celebrate just having a happy day, and that can be whatever the child chooses. If you know about the child in advance, you might contact the parent prior to the activity to discuss what would be an acceptable substitute.

Mooring Lines:

Barrett, Joyce Durham. *Willie's Not the Hugging Kind.* HarperCollins Children's. 1989.

Carle, Eric. *The Mixed-up Chameleon.* Harper & Row. 1984.

Harmin, Merrill. *Got to be Me.* Tabor. 1976.

Howe, James. *I Wish I Were a Butterfly.* Harcourt. 1987.

Polland, Barbara Kay. *Feelings Inside You & Outloud Too.* Celestial Arts. 1975.

Root, Phyllis. *Gretchen's Grandma.* Raintree. 1983.

Sendak Maurice. *Where the Wild Things Are.* HarperCollins. 1988.

Waber, Bernard. *Lyle and the Birthday Party.* Houghton Mifflin. 1973.

Wilhelm, Hans. *A Cool Kid—Like Me!* Crown. 1990.

Wright, Betty. *I Like Being Alone.* Raintree. 1981.

Zolotow, Charlotte. *Say It.* Greenwillow. 1980.

Guess Who I Am

Objectives:

Drawing reasonable conclusions from information provided

Awareness of self-image

Materials:

5 x 8 index cards, pencils.

Procedure:

1. Tell the children that they are going to make cards for a new class guessing game, called "Guess Who I Am." As an example, ask them who wears a red and blue suit, flies through the air, and can do fantastic feats—Superman!! "Right! I have just described Superman and you guessed who he was." Point out that you used three phrases to describe Superman; you are going to ask them to do the same thing to describe characters, either real or imagined, whom they know.

2. Ask the children to think of someone and then three things that describe that person. Ask for a volunteer to give the three descriptive phrases, writing them on the board. Ask the children to guess who it may be. When this has been accomplished, (you may need to do it a few times so that children get the idea), hand out the index cards.

3. Ask the children to write three phrases describing themselves on the card, writing only on one side of the card.

4. Collect the cards and either read the descriptions to the class, having them guess who the person is, or shuffle and pass out the cards to the children, with each child reading a card and thereafter guessing the person's identity. If the student doesn't get the right answer open it up the class.

Closure:

"We have had an enjoyable time today guessing our identities. Remember, we have only talked about three things for each person, and we are so much more complex than that. It might be nice to take some time today and ask your friends or family members to describe themselves to you, but allow them to tell you more than three things. You might have more fun re-discovering things about people you love."

Sailing On:

If you are doing a social studies or literature unit, you can prepare cards with characters' descriptions written on them, and proceed in the same manner as above, with the children guessing the characters described.

Mooring Lines:

Barrett, Joyce Durham. *Willie's Not the Hugging Kind.* HarperCollins Children's . 1989.

Blume, Judy. *Tales of a Fourth Grade Nothing.* Dutton. 1972.

Byars, Betsy. *Not-Just-Anybody Family.* Delacorte. 1986.

Carle, Eric. *The Mixed-up Chameleon.* Harper & Row. 1984.

Conford, Ellen. *Jenny Archer, Author.* Little, Brown. 1989.

Harmin, Merrill. *Got to be Me.* Tabor. 1976.

Hurwitz, Johanna. *Aldo Applesauce.* Morrow. 1979.

Marton, Jinina. *I'll Do it Myself.* Firefly. 1989.

Peet, Bill. *The Whingdingdilly.* Houghton Mifflin. 1977.

VanLaan, Nancy. *Rainbow Crow.* Random House. 1989.

White, E.B. *Charlotte's Web.* HarperCollins. 1952.

Yashima, Taro. *Crow Boy.* Viking. 1955.

Yorinks, Arthur. *It Happened in Pinsk.* Farrar. 1983.

Question Game

Objectives:

Oral expression of personal experiences

Awareness of feelings of self and others

Materials:

Question cards (page 70).

Procedure:

1. Sit with students in a circle.

2. Explain, "Today we are going to play a question game. The rules are simple: There are questions on cards for you to answer aloud. There are no right or wrong answers. If you don't want to answer a question, you may put the card back and choose another card. Does everyone understand?"

3. Have the deck of cards ready, and let children take turns choosing and answering cards. As each child answers, respond actively with positive comments, and thank the child for sharing. Occasionally ask, "Has anyone ever felt that way also?" or, "I have felt that way, too, sometimes."

Closure:

"It is not always easy to share how we feel. Sometimes we are afraid what others will think about us if we tell them how we really feel. But the only way people will know what is really happening inside of us is to tell them, and then others can be of help to us. This is true of people at school and at home as well."

Sailing On:

Be sure that each child in the circle has a chance to choose a card and answer.

In addition to the questions printed here, you may add questions of your own that you feel are relevant for your class, or invite students to develop questions.

You may use this exercise many times throughout the year with the same or different questions. Children can use the cards in small groups on their own.

Rosemarie Scotti Hughes, Ph.D. & Pamela C. Kloeppel, Ed.D.

Question Cards

(Cut out and tape on index cards)

If you could be anyone that you wanted to be, who would you be?	When was the last time you cried?
If you could live anywhere in the world, where would that be?	If you had your choice, what age would you be?
If you could play any musical instrument that you chose, what would you like to play?	Name one thing that makes your mother or teacher or friend angry.
If you could be a sports star, which sport would you choose?	What is one thing that you would like everyone to know about you?
What would you do with one million dollars?	Name one thing that you are afraid of.
If you could make any wish for the world, what would it be?	What is your favorite free time activity?
What is the worst thing that ever happened to you?	What do you like best about school?
What is the best thing that ever happened to you?	Do you think that TV is good or bad for children?
What is the most embarrassing situation you can remember?	What are some things that your brothers or sisters do that you get angry about?
What would you do if you could become invisible?	If you could have any job in the world when you are an adult, what would that job be?
What punishment do you dislike the most?	

Mooring Lines:

Blos, Joan. *Old Henry*. Morrow. 1987.

Byars, Betsy. *Not-Just-Anybody Family*. Delacorte. 1986.

Byars, Betsy. *The 18th Emergency*. Viking. 1973.

Cleary, Beverly. *Dear Mr. Henshaw*. Morrow. 1983.

Danziger, Paula. *Everyone Else's Parents Said Yes*. Delacorte. 1989.

Fitzhugh, Louise. *Harriet the Spy*. Harper & Row. 1964.

Giff, Patricia Reilly. *Today was a Terrible Day*. Viking. 1980.

Green, Constance. *Isabelle Shows Her Stuff*. Viking. 1984.

King-Smith, Dick. *Pigs Might Fly*. Viking. 1982.

Lionni, Leo. *Tico and the Golden Wings*. Knopf. 1987.

MacLachlan, Patricia. *Sarah, Plain and Tall*. Harper & Row. 1985.

Prelutsky, Jack. *My Parents Think I'm Sleeping*. Greenwillow. 1985.

Shreve, Susan. *Bad Dreams of a Good Girl*. Random House. 1982.

Silverstein, Shel. *Where the Sidewalk Ends*. HarperCollins. 1974.

Viorst, Judith. *Alexander and the Terrible, Horrible, No Good, Very Bad Day*. Atheneum. 1972.

**Self-Esteem
Fourth Grade Session Two**

Survey

Objectives:

Writing of scientific data

Awareness of similarities among classmates

Materials:

Chalkboard and chalk or chart paper and markers; a copy of the survey for each child (page 72), a large copy of the survey on board or chart paper.

Procedure:

1. Ask the children if they know what a survey is. You may choose to have someone look it up in the dictionary and read the definition to the class. Then ask how surveys are used (some children may mention a road or land tract survey; that is correct, it is simply another type of survey). Children might say it is a set of questions to determine public opinion, to find out preferences of consumers, voters, and so forth.

2. Explain that today they are going to complete a class survey to find out what kinds of things they have in common. Hand out the surveys to each child, and instruct them to circle YES or NO for each question.

3. When the children have finished, tally the answers (take a show of hands for each question) on the board or chart paper.

4. When the tally is complete, determine in which areas the students are most alike, or most divided. Ask the students to write a composition about the survey results. They may write their feelings about being like or different from most people in the class, being surprised by any result, or just a description of the survey results.

Closure:

Have the volunteers read their compositions aloud. Display the survey results in the room.

Sailing On:

You may want to use this survey to discuss similarities and differences of students in the class. You may also want to repeat the survey with questions more tailored to your class, and use tallying results as part of a math lesson, with percentages and fractions.

Mooring Lines:

Gray, Nigel. *A Country Far Away*. Orchard. 1988.

Spier, Peter. *People*. Doubleday. 1980.

Steele, Philip. *The People Atlas*. Oxford University. 1991.

Wolf, Bernard. *Anna's Silent World*. Lippincott. 1977.

Fourth Grade Survey Questions

YES	NO	
❏	❏	1. Do you blush?
❏	❏	2. Are you left-handed?
❏	❏	3. Do you bite your fingernails?
❏	❏	4. Do you wear glasses?
❏	❏	5. Are you wearing shoes with laces?
❏	❏	6. Do you have freckles?
❏	❏	7. Do you have allergies?
❏	❏	8. Do you have curly hair?
❏	❏	9. Are you a girl?
❏	❏	10. Do you have any brothers?
❏	❏	11. Do you have any sisters?
❏	❏	12. Are you the only child in your family?
❏	❏	13. Do you play a musical instrument
❏	❏	14. Are you wearing jeans?
❏	❏	15. Did you move to this school from another place?

Rosemarie Scotti Hughes, Ph.D. & Pamela C. Kloeppel, Ed.D.

Self-Esteem
Fourth Grade Session Three

Family Symbols

Objectives:

Expression of symbols in written form

Recognition of special qualities in one's own family

Materials:

Papers with outlines of shield, crest, and totem pole (pages 74-76), lined paper, crayons/markers, pencils.

Procedure:

1. Ask the children if they know what a "family crest" is. If you have some pictures or examples of crests, it would be helpful to show them. Explain that a crest had illustrations to tell others about a family; illustrations were often symbols or pictures that meant something else. For example, the golden arches at McDonald's do not mean that the store sells arches, but those arches represent McDonald's to us. Discuss other symbols with which the children may be familiar—some ads and logos from magazines would help illustrate the concept.

2. Explain that in medieval times, knights carried shields with markings to show their family or kingdom. In some tribes in Africa, warriors also carried shields with markings to show tribal membership. These shields were shaped differently than medieval shields. In North America, Native Americans and Eskimos used totem poles to tell of their history.

3. "Today we are going to tell something about our families by designing our own symbol stories." Let each child choose a shield or the totem pole to use. Then discuss some symbols that the children might want to use—the number of people in the family, the occupation of parents, leisure activities, and so forth.

4. After the children have completed their shields or totems, ask them to write a paragraph explaining the meaning of each symbol and why this symbol represents their family.

Closure:

"We have many similarities and differences in all of our families, but we all are important in our community and in our world."

Sailing On:

Have the children read their paragraphs to each other.

Display drawings and paragraphs around the room.

You may want to complete this activity in several steps.

Mooring Lines:

Gidel, Sonia & Gidal, Tom. *My Village in Ghana*. Pantheon. 1970.

Nhuong, Huynh Quang. *The Land I Lost: Adventures of a Boy in Vietnam*. Harper & Row. 1983.

Sneve, Virginia Driving Hawk. *Jimmy Yellow Hawk*. Holiday House. 1972.

Stein, R. Conrad. *Enchantment of the World: Mexico*. Children's. 1984.

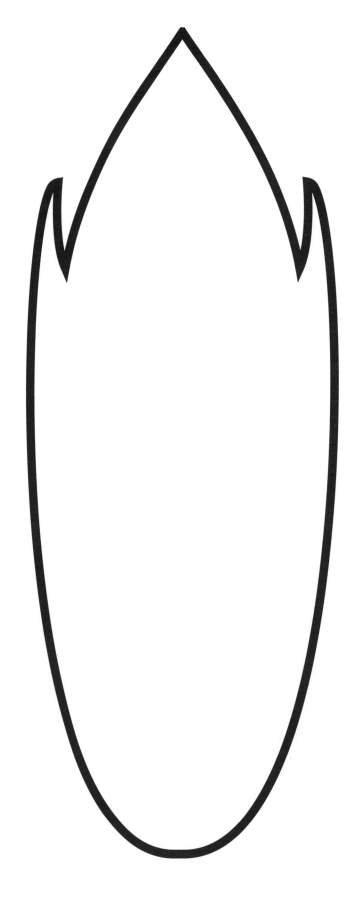

Shield

Rosemarie Scotti Hughes, Ph.D. & Pamela C. Kloeppel, Ed.D.

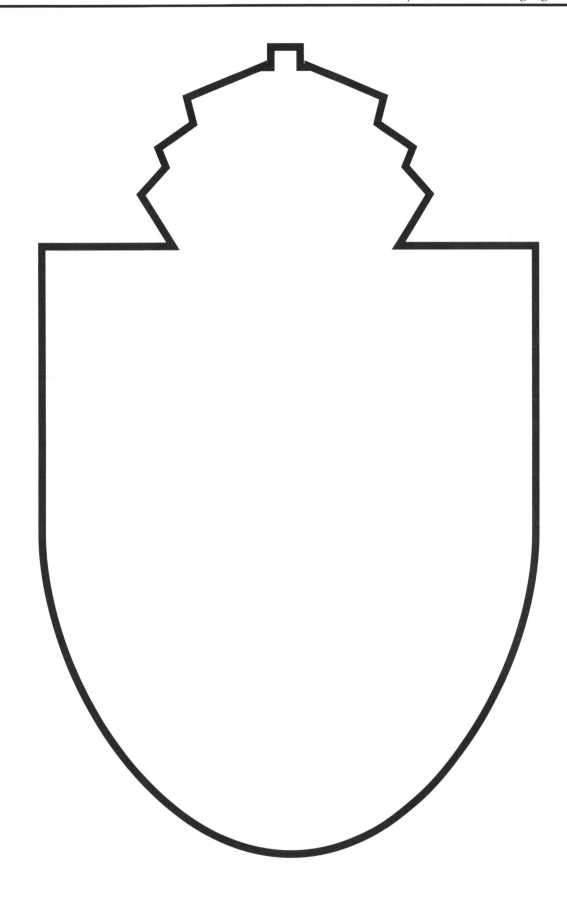

Crest

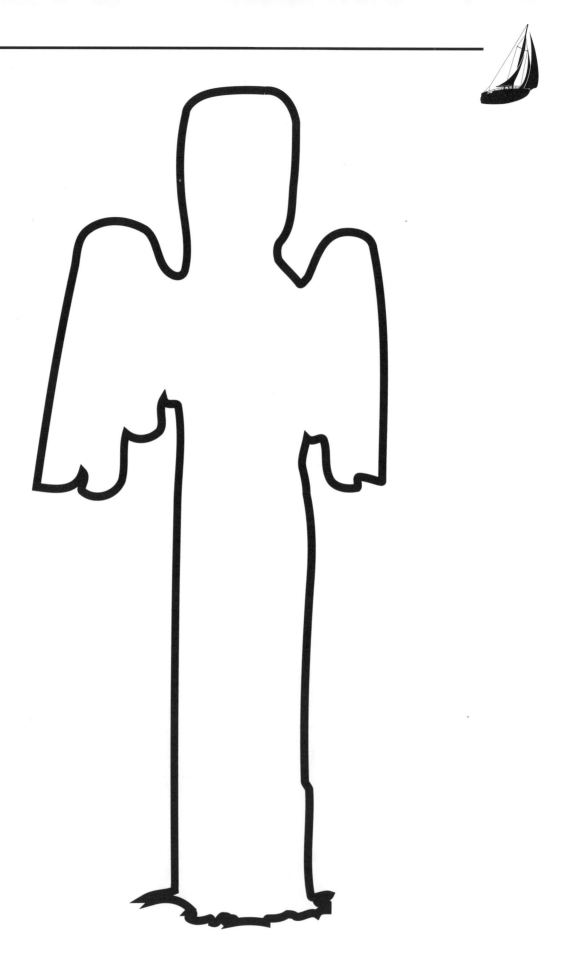

Totem

Rosemarie Scotti Hughes, Ph.D. & Pamela C. Kloeppel, Ed.D.

Self-Esteem
Fourth Grade Session Four

Olympic Medals

Objectives:

Expansion of language patterns through personal writing

Self-awareness of skills and talents

Materials:

Construction paper, scissors, crayons/markers, glue, scissors, safety pins, yarn or inexpensive ribbon, lined paper and pencils.

Procedure:

1. Ask the children if they have ever watched Olympic events on TV. Explain that the Olympics are held every two years, and describe some of the events, for both summer and winter.

2. Ask if there are any sports or other activities that they feel they do particularly well. Allow time for many children to respond. In the discussion, include things that children do well that are not sports or talent achievements, such as helping others, doing well in a particular school subject, being friendly.

3. Tell the children that today they are all going to receive an Olympic medal—medals are given only to winners, and they are all winners. "You will design your own medal, to show something that you do particularly well."

4. When the children have completed making their medals (cutting them, putting on ribbons, wearing them), assign a composition about their medals, describing what they did to earn them.

Closure:

Have each child stand up and display the medal, naming what it symbolizes. Have the class applaud each child.

Sailing On:

It is important that each child name an area of accomplishment. Those who cannot may need some recognition by you of something special they do; go around the room while drawing is going on to see if you can be of help.

You may want to take time to give a brief history of the Olympic games.

You can combine this with a social studies lesson by locating on the map/globe where past Olympic games have been held, and where future games will be held.

You may also want to read stories about Olympic game competitors such as Jim Thorpe, Jesse Owens, and Mary Lou Retton.

Mooring Lines:

Aaseng, Nathan. *Great Summer Olympic Moments*. Lerner. 1990.

Milton, Joyce. *Greg Louganis: Driving for Gold*. Random House. 1989.

Tatlow, Peter. *The Olympics*. Bookwright. 1988.

Silent Movies

Objectives:

Non-verbal dramatizations

Expression of feelings

Materials:

Role-play cards (page 79).

Procedure:

1. Ask the children to tell you how they feel when:
   —it's time to get up for school in the morning
   —time to go home from school
   —they fall and get hurt
   —they receive a nice gift.

2. Then explain, "Today we are not going to only talk about experiences that we all have, we are going to show how we feel, without words. We are going to use our whole bodies. If we had a camera, or VCR, we would be making a silent movie. We will be using pantomime."

3. Ask the children to tell what a mime does, if they do not know, have someone read dictionary definitions of mime and pantomime.

4. Pair the children. If you have an odd number, three children can work with some coaching from you. Explain that each team will choose a card, and act it out without speaking. (Some scenarios will require more set-up time than others, and you may have to talk the children through.) Have someone read the card to the class before the role-play begins.

Closure:

Discuss how it felt not being able to use words. Was it easy to show others the story? Explain that our words are actually a very small part of our communicating with others (20%); our body language tells a lot about how we feel (80%).

Sailing On:

Some children may be more skilled in pantomime than others. Give extra help where needed. Better to over-exaggerate than have children not experience the drama.

You may add whatever role play situations you wish and create cards.

You may repeat the role plays with different teams, to allow children to act the situations out in another way.

Have the children repeat the role plays with words.

If you have VCR equipment, it would be fun to video the children doing these role plays and allow them to watch themselves.

Rosemarie Scotti Hughes, Ph.D. & Pamela C. Kloeppel, Ed.D.

Mooring Lines:

Anno, Mitsumasa. *Anno's Journey*. Philomel. 1978.

Bang, Molly. *The Grey Lady and the Strawberry Snatcher*. Four Winds. 1980.

Day, Alexandra. *Good Dog, Carl*. Green Tiger. 1985.

Schories, Pat. *Mouse Around*. Farrar, Straus, Giroux. 1991.

Fourth Grade Silent Movies

Cut out and staple or glue role plays onto individual index cards:.

You are walking down the hall at school and someone pushes you.	You are late for school and your mother is telling you to hurry and finish dressing.
You get caught passing a note and the teacher reads it.	Your teacher tells you that you made 100 on the spelling test.
You drop your books on the way to class and someone helps you pick them up.	Your friend says that you cannot come into his house to play because another friend is there.
Someone teases you about the shoes you are wearing.	Your younger brother breaks your favorite toy.
Someone forgets his lunch money and you share your lunch.	Your mother tells you that you cannot go outside to play because you have to watch the baby.
Your friend asks you to go to a theme park with her family.	

Up Up and Away

Objectives:

Written and oral language skills

Self-expression of interests

Materials:

Page with outline of balloon (page 81), crayons/markers.

Procedure:

1. Explain to the class that today they are going to pretend that they will be taking a trip in a hot air balloon. Ask if anyone knows how a hot air balloon operates—there is no engine; it is dependent upon air currents; and a heater expands the air in the balloon causing it to rise.

2. If you have some pictures of hot air balloons, display them in the room. Point out the different balloon designs and colors.

3. Explain that each person will design a balloon that tells something about himself or herself. A person who likes music might use instruments and notes in the design; a person interested in sports might use some sports equipment, and so forth. Generate a brief discussion so that the children have a clear idea of the task.

4. When the balloons are decorated, have each child complete the following opening sentence and write a composition : "I would like to travel to _____ in my balloon because_____."

Closure:

"Some of us may actually get to take a trip to some of the places we desire, and some of us may never get to these places except in our minds." Lead the children into a discussion of how books can take us to many places that we will only be able to travel to in our imaginations.

Sailing On:

If you have the music for "Up Up and Away" (originally by the Fifth Dimension) play it for the class at the beginning of this session.

This is an opportunity to introduce "Around the world in 80 Days," which begins with a balloon ride. You could also show the video "To Fly," produced by the Smithsonian Institute, which opens with ballooning. Also, you could include a story on the first balloon flight in France.

Ask volunteers to read their stories to the class and tell about the decorations on their balloons.

Display balloons and stories in the room.

Mooring Lines:

Costanzo, Christie. *Hot Air Ballooning*. Capstone. 1991.

Dubois, William Pene. *The Twenty One Balloons*. Viking. 1975.

Lamorisse, Albert. *The Red Balloon*. Creative Education. 1990. (Video 34 min.).

Scarry, Huck. *Balloon Trip: A Sketchbook*. Prentice-Hall. 1983.

I Am Terrific

Objectives:

Using appropriate communication skills

Recognition of strengths in self and others

Materials:

White or colored paper folded in half (top to bottom).

Procedures:

1. Ask the children to think about famous people whom they admire, and what it is specifically that they admire. Ask the students to tell you about these people and describe them—have some "names" ready in case children get stuck (current or past presidents, well-known historical figures, or people in your school or local community that the children should know).

2. Explain that people do not have to be celebrities to be worthy of admiration—ask them to think of people among their family and friends whom them admire and the qualities those persons have.

3. Next tell them that even though they may never be famous, they still have qualities and talents that are special, that no one else has. Hand out the paper. With the fold at the top, the children are to draw a picture of themselves. When they open the paper, they are to write "I am terrific" across the top. On the top half, they are to complete the sentence, "What I like best about myself is...." On the bottom segment, "What I do best is...."

Closure:

"It is important to keep in mind what you do best. Often, as adults, what we enjoy doing and do best as a child becomes part of the career we will have as an adult. It is O.K. not to be "best" at everything. No adult is good at everything. What is important is that you pay attention to what makes you special and unique, to try your best in all areas, but to accept that no one is perfect!"

Sailing On:

If children are asked to tell something positive about themselves they often have difficulty—writing it is easier.

If there are still some children who cannot find positive things to say about themselves, enlist the aid of classmates, or give children some positive comments.

Have children read their statements to the class.

Mooring Lines:

Aaseng, Nathan. *Bruce Jenner.* Lerner. 1979.

McKnown, Robin. *Heroic Nurses.* GP Putnam's Sons. 1966.

Washington, Rosemary. *Mary Lou Retton: "The Achievers."* Lerner. 1985.

Rosemarie Scotti Hughes, Ph.D. & Pamela C. Kloeppel, Ed.D.

Self-Esteem
Fifth Grade Session Two

Wheel of Fortune

Objectives:

Vocabulary building and sentence writing

Recognition of personal strengths

Materials:

Two-sided wheel handout (pages 84-85).

Procedure:

1. "When you filled in your "Terrific" papers, you wrote down what you liked about yourself and something that you did very well. Today we are going to think more good things about ourselves. Today we are going to write down six good qualities we each have— these qualities are called 'strengths' (write word on board)." Have a student read the definition of "strengths" from the dictionary.

2. Under the word "strengths" have students develop a list of strengths that people possess.

3. Hand out wheels to the students. Instruct them to write one of their strengths on each section of the wheel.

4. Next, have them turn the wheels over, and write a sentence about each strength on the reverse side of the section. The sentence should tell how the student evidences that strength in daily life.

Closure:

When all have finished, ask a child to stand and name one strength. Then invite all who listed that strength to stand. Have that group sit down and proceed with next child. Be sure to include all children. Point out the strengths that everyone possesses in this room.

Sailing On:

Have the students create a paragraph about one of their strengths. You may have to help the children generate strengths and to spell them correctly using dictionaries.

Display the wheels around the room.

Mooring Lines:

McWhirter, Norris & McWhirter, Ross. *Guiness Book of Surprising Accomplishments*. Sterling. 1979.

Kalb, Jonah & Viscott, David. *What Every Kid Should Know*. Sensitivity Games. 1976.

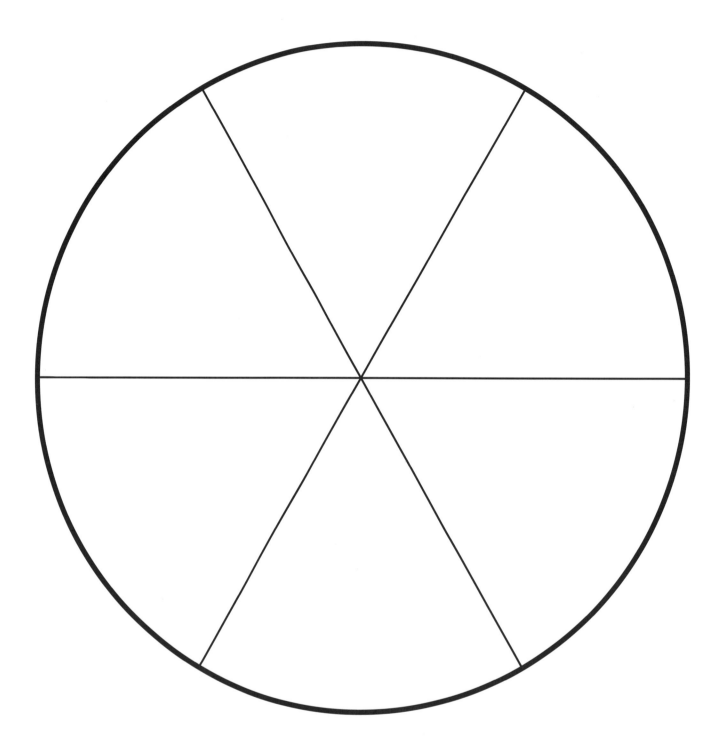

Rosemarie Scotti Hughes, Ph.D. & Pamela C. Kloeppel, Ed.D.

How I Show My Strengths

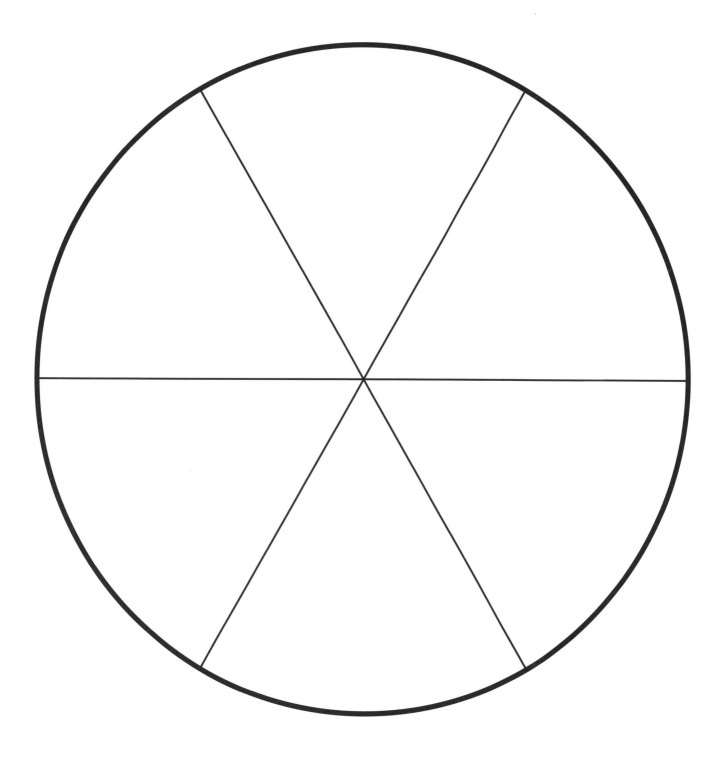

Butterfly

Objectives:

Composition writing

Self-awareness of ability to change

Materials:

Outline of butterfly (page 87), crayons/markers, scissors.

Procedure:

1. Review briefly the life-cycle of the butterfly. Explain that a beautiful butterfly must first break out of a dark cocoon to be able to spread its wings and fly. "Sometimes it is as though we are in a cocoon, either not using the talents and skills we possess, or keeping bad habits which prevent us from being free like butterflies."

2. "Think of something about yourself that you would like to change. For example, you might want to be a more helpful person, or perhaps to spend more time on your homework, or to stop biting your nails."

3. "On the back of the butterfly, write something that you would like to change about yourself, or a goal that you would like to achieve. Then color and cut out your butterfly, and we will display them around the room to remind you of your goal."

4. Ask the students to share what they have written. Allow this sharing to be voluntary only. Some children may not want to tell others what they want to change.

Closure:

Explain that making change is always hard, for children and adults. Ask what the benefits of making change are, and what are some of the problems associated with change. Often, problems include others not liking the changes. Another is that changes often take a long time—it takes at least 8 weeks to change a habit like nail biting. "It takes courage to change, just as it takes courage for the butterfly to leave the cocoon."

Sailing On:

Ask the children to think of how they could go about reaching their goal. What steps would they have to take? Ask them to write a composition about how they will make changes in their lives.

Mooring Lines:

Blume, Judy. *Freckle Juice.* MacMillan. 1971.
Blume, Judy. *Tales of a Fourth Grade Nothing.* Dell. 1972.
Coatsworth, Elizabeth. *Marra's World.* Greenwillow. 1975.
Rosenberg, Maxine. *Growing Up Adopted.* Bradbury. 1989.

Rosemarie Scotti Hughes, Ph.D. & Pamela C. Kloeppel, Ed.D.

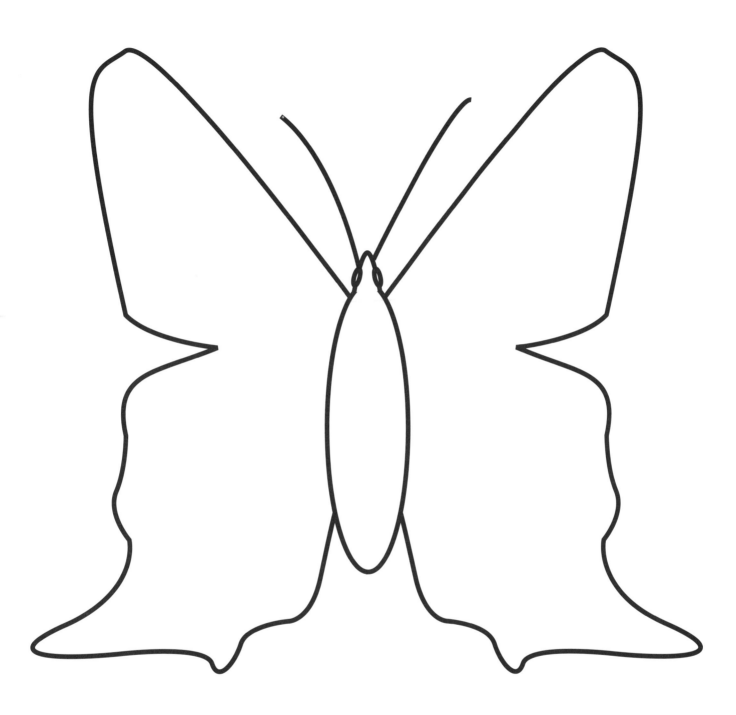

Haiku Writing

Objectives:

Creative language experience through poetry writing

Self-assessment and self expression

Materials:

Pencils and paper.

Procedure:

1. "Today we are going to write poems about ourselves. They are very special poems call HAIKU. This is a poem that originated in Japan, and it does not rhyme. It has a very special form: It only has three lines. The first line has five syllables the second line seven syllables, and the third line five syllables."

2. Clap out the rhythm of the poem with the children.

3. If you have some examples of Haiku, read them to the class; if not, compose a Haiku about yourself, and put it on the board.

   You may use this example:
   "I am a teacher.
   I like to be with children.
   It feels good to me."

4. "When you write your haiku, it must follow the 5-7-5 form, and it must be about you."

5. Ask for volunteers to share their writing.

Closure:

Have a few minutes of discussion about whether or not it was difficult to choose what to write about and also keep it within a certain form. Reflect with children that life itself presents some limits to us, and we often have to choose how we will feel about ourselves in certain limiting situations, i.e., we may have not achieved top grades, not because we didn't work hard, but for some reason just didn't make it. Should we feel bad about who we are because of it?

Sailing On:

You might discuss what children would say about themselves before beginning the actual composing.

First conduct some group haiku poetry composing, and then do the individual writing in a second session.

Mooring Lines:

Atwood, Ann. *Fly With the Wind Flow With the Water.* Charles Scribner's. 1979.

Behn, Harry. *Cricket Songs.* Harcourt. 1964.

Cassedy, Sylvia & Suetake, Kunihiro. *Birds, Frogs, and Moonlight.* Doubleday. 1962.

Tames, Richard. *Journey Through Japan.* Troll. 1991.

Self-Esteem
Fifth Grade Session Five

Mirror, Mirror

Objectives:

Paragraph construction

Setting goals for oneself

Materials:

"Mirror, Mirror" handout (page 90).

Procedure:

1. If possible, have the children seated in a circle.

2. "This is your last year in an elementary school. Next year you will be going to middle school, then on to high school. After that, you will be considered as an adult. Have you ever thought about what you will look like next year, in middle school, in five years, in high school, or as an adult?"

3. Discuss possible changes in appearance.

4. Next, discuss what they will be doing next year, then in five years, then ten years from now. This discussion could take the entire time, or just a few minutes, depending upon the interest and imagination/skills of the children.

5. The next step, which can be done in a following session, would be to draw pictures of themselves in the mirrors in the appropriate places, showing what they will look like and also be doing.

Closure:

It isn't easy to think about the future, because it seems so far away. When we think about what we could possibly do in the future, we are setting some goals for ourselves. It is easier to stay focused on what we are about—for us, doing well in school—when we have some goal in sight.

Mooring Lines:

Hall, Lynn. *Uphill All the Way*. Charles Scribner's Sons. 1984.

Landis, James David. *The Sisters Impossible*. Alfred A. Knopf. 1979.

Shockley, Robert & Cutlip, Glen. *Careers in Teaching*. Rosen. 1988.

Strang, Celia. *Foster Mary*. McGraw Hill. 1979.

Walter, Mildred Pitts. *Justin and the Best Biscuits in the World*. Lothrop, Lee & Shepard. 1986.

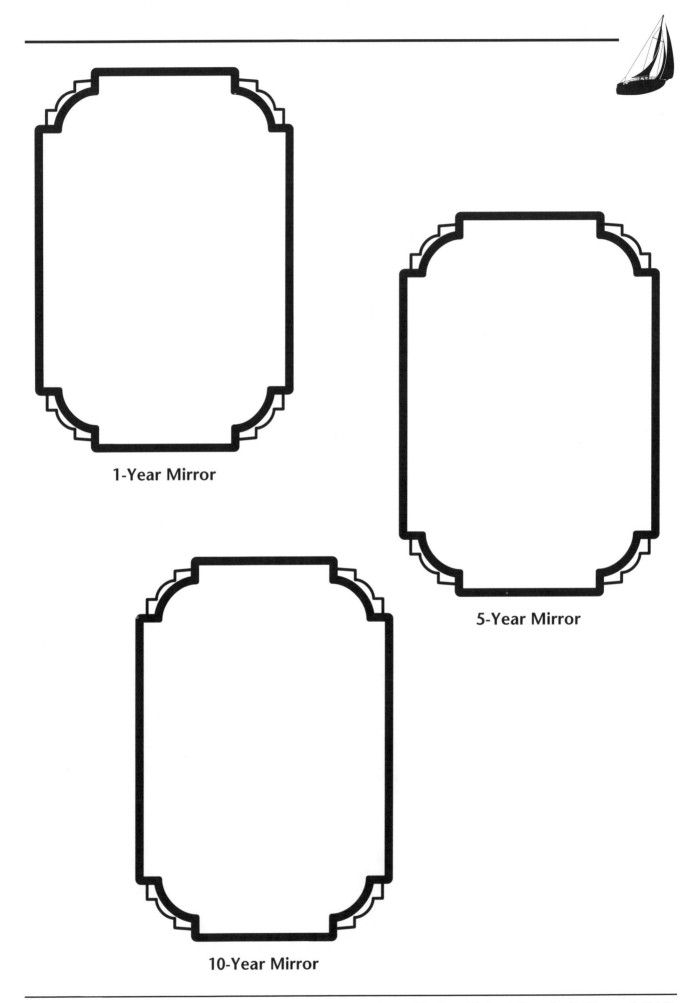

1-Year Mirror

5-Year Mirror

10-Year Mirror

Rosemarie Scotti Hughes, Ph.D. & Pamela C. Kloeppel, Ed.D.

Self-Esteem
Fifth Grade Session Six

Storytime

Objectives:

Developing added meaning to a literary character
Self-appraisal

Materials:

Paper and pencils.

Procedure:

1. Ask the children to think about a book that they read recently. Then, think about a specific character in that book.

2. Lead a discussion about the favorite characters. Include the following:

   — Why did you like the character?

   — Could you see yourself in the character?

   — Did the character have any qualities that you would like to have?

   — Are there any characteristics in the character that you would like to change?

   — Are there any characteristics you both share?

3. Explain to the children that they are now to write a composition about this character, explaining how the character *IS* and *IS NOT* like themselves.

   Format to use:

   1. Book title

   2. Author

   3. Name of character and role in the story

   4. Paragraph beginning, "I am like _____ because _____"

   5. Paragraph beginning, "I am unlike _____ because _____"

Sailing On:

You may want to assign specific biographical or fictional works be read before doing this exercise.

Mooring Lines:

Use any books available in your classroom or school library.

Notes:

Rosemarie Scotti Hughes, Ph.D. & Pamela C. Kloeppel, Ed.D.

Decision Making

Introduction

Children believe that life "just happens." They are not aware that they make many decisions daily. They are not aware that when they do nothing about a situation, they are still making a decision. Children need decision-making skills to make informed choices and be prepared for complex decisions that will come later in their lives. They need to realize that they are responsible for what happens to them.

The goal of this unit is for students to learn the steps of decision making, and to understand it as a skill which can be improved by practice. The lessons can be applied to individual and school situations, for both current problem solving and the prevention of future problems.

Four models of decision making are given. For Kindergarten through Second Grade the model is very simple: *"First Think, Second Act."* For grades three through five there are three models, each listed below, so that you can use them with the class as you wish, depending upon which best suits the needs of the class: "D.O.G.," "D.E.C.I.D.E.," and "S.A.I.L."

D.O.G. Model of Decision Making

D: What is the Decision to be made?
O: What is the Outcome of each action I could take?
G: Go with the best outcome.

D.E.C.I.D.E. Model of Decision Making

D: What is the Decision to be made?
E: Examine possible options.
C: Consider the consequences of each option.
I: Identify the Ideal solution.
D: Do it
E: Evaluate it

S.A.I.L. Model of Decision Making

S: What is the problem to be Solved?
A: Look at All possible options.
I: Identify the Ideal solution.
L: Look at the consequences.

What If

Objectives:

Develop listening and speaking skills

Identify logical consequences of daily decisions

Materials:

3 X 5 colored index cards or sheets of colored paper cut in quarters (4 different colors); on each card or paper tape or staple one "What If" phrase (see end of lesson).

Procedure:

1. Begin by asking children, "What happens when you turn on a light switch?" "When you pour too much milk into a glass?" "When you forget to feed a pet?" Explain that what happens is called a consequence.

2. Now introduce the class to the game called, "What if...." Place cards upside down so phrases do not show. Have a student identify a desired color. The teacher then reads the situation on the card of this color to the student, asking first "What would happen if...," The student answers.

3. Extend the discussion by asking if the student were ever in such a situation and what happened.

Closure:

"We agreed today that our actions cause things to happen. When we call someone a name, they may get angry. When we eat too much candy we can get sick. We also learned that even when we do not act, we can cause things to happen; when we don't go to bed on time, we are tired the next day. When we don't eat, we get hungry. Our decisions can result in good or bad consequences. All our actions have consequences."

Sailing On:

You can add situations of your own to the "What If" phrase list, tailoring situations to areas of needed improvement of your class. You might also ask the children to make up situations.

Mooring Lines:

Asch, Frank. *Goodbye House*. Prentice Hall. 1986.

Barrett, Judith. *What's Left?* Atheneum. 1983.

Seuss, Dr. *Hop on Pop*. Random House. 1963.

Seuss, Dr. *If I Ran the Circus.*. Random House. 1956.

Seuss, Dr. *McElligot's Pool*. Random House. 1975.

Rosemarie Scotti Hughes, Ph.D. & Pamela C. Kloeppel, Ed.D.

"What If" Phrases

You forget to feed a pet	You do not come straight home after school
You don't share a toy	You go to a friend's house without telling an adult
You call someone a name	You hit someone
You help mother dry the dishes	You get into a fight
You share a treat with a friend	You tell a lie
You are kind to someone	You talk to a stranger
You don't brush your teeth	You leave your lunch ticket at home
You eat too much candy	You give someone a hug
You eat fruits and vegetables	You lose your mother in a store while shopping

Decision Making
Kindergarten Session Two

What's the Scoop?

Objectives:

Oral reporting in class

Practice application of decision making

Materials:

Copy of an empty ice cream cone handout (page 97) for each student, crayons or markers.

Procedure:

1. Ask the children if they like ice cream and why. Ask them to tell their favorite ice cream flavors. Discuss the ingredients that make the ice cream taste so good—chocolate chips, nuts, fruit, flavorings, color, and so forth.

2. Ask, "Has anyone ever thought about an ice cream flavor that no one has made?" Give the students sufficient time to generate many exotic flavor suggestions. (These do not have to make sense: apple-chocolate-watermelon would be fine.)

3. Hand out the ice cream cone sheet and ask the children to draw their made-up ice cream flavor on the empty cone, showing "chunks" of the flavoring.

4. When they are finished, have each student stand and tell the name of their made-up flavor and why they selected it.

5. Now ask the group how new flavors are "invented" at the ice cream store? How do the ice cream makers decide whether or not to sell this new flavor? How do they know if other people will like it?

Closure:

"We learned today that some of us like ice cream but some of us don't. New ice cream flavors are thought out in advance before they go on sale. The ice cream maker sells ice cream only after thinking about the taste and trying out the flavor to see if it tastes good. Sometimes ice cream makers even have trial markets for several months to test whether people will buy the flavor. Just as ice cream sellers think carefully about their new ice cream flavors, we too need to think about our actions before we act. We need to think, is this good for me? Is it good for others? When we think before we act, our actions are better; we are able to do more.

Sailing On:

If some children have trouble "inventing" a flavor, tell them to use their favorite flavor.

This lesson could be followed by a trip to an ice cream store or a visitor from an ice cream store or a fast food chain, to discuss trial markets and new creations. Emphasis should always be on the decision making process.

Mooring Lines:

Black, Irma Simonton. *Is This My Dinner?* Albert Whitman. 1972.

Hines, Anna Grossnickle. *Daddy Makes the Best Spaghetti.* Clarion. 1986.

Seuss, Dr. *On Beyond Zebra.* Random House. 1955.

Rosemarie Scotti Hughes, Ph.D. & Pamela C. Kloeppel, Ed.D.

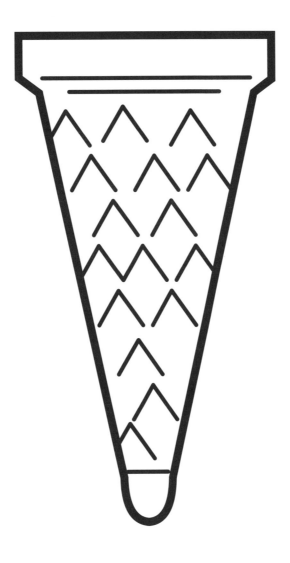

Decision Making
Kindergarten Session Three

Three Helping Hands

Objectives:

Oral reporting to the class

Identify reasons for and consequences of decisions

Materials:

Large sheet of drawing paper, folded in half, for each student; sufficient crayons or markers.

Procedure:

1. Ask the children to look at their hands. "Think of all of the things that you do each day with your hands. Who can name some things that you do with your hands?"

2. Discuss with children that sometimes hands can help others; sometimes hands hurt others. Ask how their hands have ***helped*** others. After examples are given ask how they have ***hurt*** others with their hands. Ask them "How do you feel when you ***help*** others?" "How do you feel when you ***hurt*** others?" Emphasize that they can *choose* to use their hands to help or hurt others as well as themselves; the decision to help or hurt is our own. We are responsible for what we do.

3. Distribute folded paper. Ask the children to trace their hands on one half of the paper and, in the other half, draw a time when they used their hands to help someone.

4. When students are finished, have each student stand and tell about the picture. Ask each student, "Why did you choose to help someone?" "What happened when you helped?" "How did you feel when you were a helper?"

Closure:

"We learned today that we have all helped others; each time we helped someone, we had to first make a decision before we actually gave the help. We also learned that most people like our help. So when we decide to help people we often make them happy. The result of helping others is making them, and often ourselves, happy. Lets say these steps of decision making: For Best Results: ***First, Think; Second, Act.***"

Sailing On:

Children who hurt others and "like" doing so should see the counselor individually for help or possible referral.

Have the children draw a second picture of themselves using their hands to hurt someone. Have each student explain his decision to hurt and what happened. Compare and contrast results and feelings of helping/hurting others.

Mooring Lines:

DeBrunhoff, Jean. *The Story of Babar the Little Elephant*. Random House. 1960.

Berenstein, Stan & Berenstein, Jan. *The Berenstein Bears Go to the Doctor*. Random House. 1981.

Rosemarie Scotti Hughes, Ph.D. & Pamela C. Kloeppel, Ed.D.

Decision Making
Kindergarten Session Four
What Do You Wear?

Objectives:

Sort, match, and categorize objects

Practice decision making skills

Materials:

Copies of pictures of clothing (page 100) for each child.

Procedure:

1. Talk about the weather today. Have the children discuss the weather in relations to what they wore to school today. Ask what they would have worn in other types of weather—what if it were raining, snowing, windy, hot, very cold, and so forth.

2. Distribute copies of the next page to children and ask them to decide what to wear for different weather situations. "The weather report says...." "What will you wear?" "Why?" "How did you make that choice?"

3. Ask them if they choose clothes to wear for other reasons, i.e., going to a special place, nothing else clean, because it is new, a favorite color, and so forth.

Closure:

Today we learned that certain clothes are good to wear in certain weather; a coat is good in the winter when it is cold, but bad in the summer when it is hot. Shorts are great in the summer, when it is hot, but bad when it is snowing. We learned we often decide what to wear because of the weather. We learned we make good clothing decisions when we use the facts we have about the weather. We must always use facts to make good decisions.

Sailing On:

Reverse this activity by choosing an article of clothing and asking the children what the weather would probably be if this were what they were wearing.

Use this handout to teach the alphabet; draw clothes on the board, using an overhead projector, or reproduce the pictures without words. Have students write beginning letters on each piece of clothing.

Mooring Lines:

Radlauer, Ruth Shaw. *Molly Goes Hiking*. Prentice-Hall. 1987.

Rice, Eve. *New Blue Shoes*. MacMillan. 1975.

Boots

Swim Suit

T-Shirt

Sweater

Sun Glasses

Umbrella

Earmuffs

Jacket

Scarf

Boxer Shorts

Ski Cap

Sun Hat

Mittens

Rosemarie Scotti Hughes, Ph.D. & Pamela C. Kloeppel, Ed.D.

Decision Making
Kindergarten Session Five
What Do You Say, Dear?

Objectives:

Develop listening and speaking skills
Practice decision making

Materials:

None

Procedure:

1. Begin by asking children what they usually say when someone gives them a present (thank you), when they make a request of another person (please), and when they need to walk by someone (excuse me). Explain that these are words that make other people feel good, show we are courteous and respectful, and have good manners.

2. Ask for a volunteer to respond to one of the following situations to show that he or she has good manners. Ask each volunteer to give a reason for the response given.

    You are served broccoli at dinner at a friend's house, and you do not like broccoli.

    You are asked to bring grandma a glass of milk.

    A friend asks you to a birthday party.

    You accidentally bump into someone.

    Someone bumps into you.

    You knock over your carton of milk at lunch, and it spills all over your friend.

    You see someone trip and fall.

    Your mother tells you that it is bedtime, but you want to watch more TV.

    You are called to get up for school, but you want to stay in bed.

    Your brother beats you to the bathroom in the morning.

    The teacher thinks you hit someone, but you did not.

3. After a student gives a response, ask the others to vote on the answer with a thumbs up (for appropriate) or a thumbs down (for inappropriate). After each vote determine the most popular answer. Explain that the most popular (hopefully) answer is a good-manner answer. If this is not the case, explain why the good-manner answer would be in the child's best interest.

Closure:

"There are acceptable ways to act in each situation, both at school and at home. When we decide to act in a respectful way, and use good manners, usually people will be respectful toward us. But, if we are nice and someone is still mean to us we can feel good about ourselves, because we were smart enough to use our good manners. We know we did what was right."

Sailing On:

Use the lesson in shorter sessions throughout the week, choosing only one or two good-manner decisions for each session.

Use situations specific to your classroom where children need to improve their behaviors.

Mooring Lines:

Hamilton, Morse & Hamilton, Emily. *My Name is Emily*. Greenwillow. 1979.

Hoban, Russell Conwell. *Dinner at Alberta's*. HarperCollins. 1976.

Minarik, Else Holmelund. *Little Bear's Friend*. Harper & Row. 1960.

Parish, Peggy. *Mind Your Manners*. Greenwillow. 1978.

Rosemarie Scotti Hughes, Ph.D. & Pamela C. Kloeppel, Ed.D.

Decision Making
Kindergarten Session Six

I Get to Choose

Objectives:

Oral reporting in class

Understand steps of good decision making

Materials:

Coloring paper and pencils.

Procedure:

1. Begin by asking students their favorite place to eat. Is it a fast food place (which it probably is) or a more formal restaurant? Maybe it is a relative's house.

2. Today the students have to decide on a birthday or Mother's or Father's Day celebration meal for a special adult in their life. They are to plan the food and place for this party. Remember the party is for another, not for them; therefore, decisions center on what the other person likes, not what they like.

3. Each student is to draw the place they would take this adult and the food they would order for him or her.

4. Ask for each student to stand and discuss their plans, giving their reasons for their decisions.

5. After all students have reported, ask if the place they selected for the adult is different from the place they would have selected for themselves. Is the food different? Why is there a difference?

6. Say to the children, "Before we planned this party for a special adult, we thought about what that person liked, then we made a decision. We made the decision because we knew the outcome—this person would be happy. What would have happened if we took this person to a place he or she did not like?" Let the students answer, then continue, "Before we act, we must think about the outcome—the consequence. We want the outcome to be good, so we must think about our decision before we act."

7. Write on the board: ***First, Think; Second, Act***

Closure:

"All good acts are the result of good decisions. Lets recite the steps to good decision making: ***First, Think; Second, Act.***"

Mooring Lines:

Ets, Marie Hall. *Cow's Party*. Viking. 1966.

Schick, Eleanor. *Joey on His Own*. Dial. 1982.

Decision Making
First Grade Session One
There's More Than One Way

Objectives:

Listen and follow directions

Understand that there can be more than one solution to a problem

Materials:

Chalkboard, chalk.

Procedure:

1. Explain to the children that they are going to play a game with you. They will need to listen closely and think creatively. They are to think of different ways of going from one side of the room to the other.

2. Pair children and have each pair decide on and demonstrate one way to go from one point in the room to the other. If a pair gets "stuck" and cannot think of a different way, have classmates offer a suggestion. The children may hop, skip, crawl, dance, jump, and so forth. Encourage diagonal, backwards movements, and so forth.

3. Children are to write the first letter of the method they plan to use on the board; they are to state this method; then they are to act.

4. When all pairs have gone across the room, ask if there was only one "right" way to cross the room. Let children discuss the many correct methods. Then explain that in some circumstances there is a right way to walk across the room: when the bell rings, when there is a fire alarm, when someone is hurt, when helping someone with a disability.

5. Reemphasize that often there is more than one way to do something. Different ways of doing things are often fine if you can still meet your goal and don't hurt anyone. Ask the students to give personal examples of a time when they did something different than their friends. What happened?

Closure:

"We always decide to act or not to act; it is up to us. We can decide to act the same as or differently from our friends—"to do our own thing." It is OK to be different, to go our own way if we can meet our goals and not hurt anyone. There are times, though for the safety of others and ourselves, when we can't go our own way, when we must act as everyone else acts. We make the decision to act differently or the same as others, based on the people around us and where we are. We decide on our actions."

Sailing On:

Explain that safety is important, and only allow one pair to move at a time.

Use this as an introduction to a lesson on safety on the bus or at school, emphasizing whether it is appropriate or inappropriate to act differently in certain circumstances.

Mooring Lines:

Cole, Joanna. *This is the Place for Me*. Scholastic. 1986.

Gordon, Sharon. *Drip Drop*. Troll. 1981.

Hover, Margo. *What Kind of Truck?* Western. 1983.

Ingoglia, Gina. *Tootle and Katy Caboose*. Western. 1989.

Kingsley, Emily Perl. *What do You do?* Western. 1981.

Rosemarie Scotti Hughes, Ph.D. & Pamela C. Kloeppel, Ed.D.

Decision Making
First Grade Session Two

Way To Go

Objectives:

Oral reporting

Practice decision making

Materials:

A large map of the United States, or home state, or city, or neighborhood streets; paper and pencil.

Procedure:

1. Discuss what was done in the last activity. Recall the many different ways children traveled across the room.

2. Show the map and note that people travel from one place to another in different ways. Discuss various methods of travel by asking students the ways they have traveled in the past. Include walking, bicycling, swimming, and other more typical responses. Ask the children to distinguish travel between close places, then farther places, then great distances.

3. Tell the children they have been making choices about traveling; they make travel choices each day. They choose ways to travel to places they go—school, church, the store, the movies, a friend's house, and so forth. How do they make these decisions?

4. Next ask the children if they make other choices each day; give them time to discuss such choices.

5. Then ask each child to write one word or sentence about a choice made every day.

6. Ask each student to share this choice, give the reason why this choice was made and the outcome, using the model of decision making: ***First, Think; Second, Act***

Closure:

We make many decisions each day; for each decision we must first think about all the outcomes (what can happen) before we act. Our actions should always be what is best for us and the people we care for. When we think about our actions before we act, we do better things for ourselves and others.

Sailing On:

Use an enlarged map (or transparency) of the streets and neighborhood around the school for those with more limited geographical perceptions.

To expand the session, create a group story about taking a trip, with each student adding a sentence. After completing the story ask the students to point out important decisions made during the trip. If any decisions were omitted, you should add them.

Mooring Lines:

Bond, Felicia. *Poinsettia and Her Family*. Thomas Y. Crowell Junior. 1981.

Bright, Robert. *Georgie and the Baby Birds*. Doubleday. 1983.

Disney, Walt. *Pinocchio's Promise*. Bantam. 1986.

Fleming, Ian. *Chitty, Chitty, Bang, Bang*. Knopf Books for Young Readers. 1989.

Hillert, Margaret. *Let's Have a Party*. Modern Curriculum. 1981.

Decision Making
First Grade Session Three

The Birthday Party

Objectives:

To listen and talk with each other

To understand that several different decisions must sometimes be made for a desired outcome

Materials:

Drawing paper, crayons or markers; chalkboard and chalk, or chart paper and markers.

Procedure:

1. Ask the children if they have ever been to a birthday party. Ask them what they like about a birthday party; i.e., kinds of things they like to do, the food they like to eat, the gifts they like to receive.

2. As the students respond write the following vocabulary words on the board: cake, ice cream, candy, party, present, gift, candles, fun, food, other as appropriate. Have students write them on their papers and say them aloud, and have volunteers state a complete sentence using each word.

3. Ask if students have ever planned a party; give them a chance to discuss. Explain for any event, it is necessary to PLAN. Explain what it means to plan—think ahead—then act.

4. Tell the students they are to plan a party; they must decide everything that is needed. Put a list of choices on the board; they are outlined below:

   Place: Where will you have the party? Where would you not want a party to be held?

   Time: When will you have the party?

   Friends: Whom will you invite? Whom will you not invite?

   Food: What kind of food will you serve? What kind of food will you not serve?

   Fun: What will you do at the party? What will you not do at the party?

   Money: How much can you spend?

   No Plans: What will happen if you make no plans for the party? Would the party be a success?

5. Ask the children to draw a picture of their planned birthday party. Encourage creativity and imagination—outer space, Disneyworld, a cruiseship, and so forth. You may want to discuss some possibilities before the children draw.

6. When children have drawn their pictures, let them tell about what they have drawn and tell the one decision that was most important in their plans.

 Rosemarie Scotti Hughes, Ph.D. & Pamela C. Kloeppel, Ed.D.

Closure:

Explain that before a successful party can be given many decisions must be made. Before any successful act decisions must be made: *First, Think; Second, Act.*

Sailing On:

In some religions, birthday parties are not celebrated; if this surfaces in your class allow the child to choose another type of party—beginning of school, fall, end of year and so forth.

This might be a time to plan an actual class party; perhaps you could invite another class for simple refreshments, or plan a party for mothers and/or grandmothers or other caregivers.

Instead of listing choices in #4, let students brainstorm and plan together, asking "What do we need to have at our party?" and listing items students identify.

Mooring Lines:

Chevalier, Christa. *Spence Makes Circles*. Albert Whitman. 1982.

Cooney, Nancy Evans. *The Blanket That Had To Go*. G.P. Putnam's Sons. 1981.

Hutchins, Pat. *Changes, Changes*. MacMillan. 1981.

Matthews, Morgan. *Whoo's Too Tired?* Troll. 1989.

Winnie the Pooh Birthday Book. Dutton Child. 1993.

Wood, John Norris. *Could You Be a Frog?* Ideals. 1990.

It's All in How You Say It

Objectives:

State thoughts in complete sentences

Understand how our words affect others

Materials:

None

Procedure:

1. Explain that today we will discuss how our words can make others feel good or bad. You will demonstrate and need a volunteer to help you. Tell students that you are going to do a short role play. Asking the volunteer in a rough tone of voice, "___(name)__, get the red book and bring it here." Then, when the volunteer sits down, say in a pleasant tone of voice, to the same student, "___(name)___, please bring me the red book. Thank you."

2. Ask the student how he or she felt with the first command, and then with the second. Ask which was preferred, and which request encouraged more cooperation.

3. Using the following list, read or have a student read, in an "unfriendly" tone of voice, one statement to the class. Then ask the students to re-phrase the statement so the listener will feel better and/or want to cooperate; have students use complete sentences.

> Go sit down!
>
> Shut up!
>
> Pick up that paper!
>
> Give me your milk!
>
> You cannot have it!
>
> Hey, you!
>
> I want it!
>
> Get out of my way!
>
> That is mine!
>
> You are wrong!
>
> I was here first!
>
> You cannot play!
>
> You are last!

Closure:

Each time we speak we can hurt someone by what we say and the way we say it. If we think about what we say *before* we say it, we can make people feel better. When you are nice to others they are usually nice to you.

Rosemarie Scotti Hughes, Ph.D. & Pamela C. Kloeppel, Ed.D.

Sailing On:

Discuss how each statement makes the *speaker* feel.

Write each statement on a colored index card and allow children to choose phrases.

You might want to add some negative statements that you have heard the students use in the classroom.

Mooring Lines:

Cosgrove, Stephen. *Sassafras.* Price Stern Sloan. 1988.

Martin, Melanie. *Itsy-Bitsy Giant.* Troll. 1989.

Muller, Romeo. *Puff in the Land of the Living Lies.* My. 1982.

Peck, Pauline C. *Play Ball, Buddy!* Field. 1989.

Reece, James H. *Letter and Clyde.* Scholastic. 1991.

Fantasy Furnishings

Objectives:

Expand writing, speaking and vocabulary skills

Practice decision making

Materials:

Drawing paper, crayons, markers, magazines, scissors, glue, tape.

Procedure:

1. Ask the students to think about what they would like to have in their bedrooms. They can have anything they wish; they can create real or imaginary rooms. Discuss some ideas that the students may have. You can encourage thinking by a "brainstorming" session.

2. Ask the students to draw their fantasy rooms or to cut out pictures from magazines for their rooms. Remind them that anything goes— trees, oceans, cars, and so forth; all are O.K.

3. When the students have completed their pictures, ask them to describe their bedrooms, telling why they chose to furnish the room as they did.

4. Write key descriptive words on the board given by the students that you want to use as vocabulary words. Have students recite and define these.

5. Ask the students, "In real life, not your dream world, who decides what your bedroom will be like? Who chooses your furniture? pictures? toys? books?" Help students explore these questions by explaining that there are always limits on our choices, such as parents making certain decisions about the room, having to share with another person(s), not having enough money for all the things desired.

6. Ask the students, "In real life, how can you change one thing in your room to make it more like you want it to be?" What decisions do you have to make? Can you talk to your parents about this change? Ask for volunteers to share their desired changes, and some steps they can take to make changes.

Rosemarie Scotti Hughes, Ph.D. & Pamela C. Kloeppel, Ed.D.

Closure:

"Our real worlds always have limits, but we can still make changes if we want to. Changes may be small but each change requires decision-making and planning: *First, Think; Second, Act.*"

Sailing On:

In *brainstorming* it is important to list all ideas, no matter how outrageous or impossible. Ideas are not critiqued at this time. After all ideas are brainstormed, pluses and minuses of each item/option are evaluated and the best one is chosen. In this exercise critiquing is not needed because the students are dealing in fantasy.

Have the children draw pictures of their actual room and their desired room.

Mooring Lines:

Hayes, Geoffrey. *Patrick Buys a Coat.* Alfred A. Knopp. 1985.

Reece, James H. *Letter and Clyde.* Scholastic. 1991.

Cooney, Nancy Evans. *The Blanket that had to Go.* G.P. Putnam's Sons. 1981.

Cosgrove, Stephen. *Sassafras.* Price, Stern, Sloan. 1988.

Matthews, Morgan. *Whoo's too Tired?* Troll. 1989.

School is For Me

Objectives:

Practice speaking and writing skills

Understand that decisions should result in more good consequences than bad

Materials:

Paper and pencil, chalk and chalkboard.

Procedure:

1. Ask each student to write down one thing they like about school, e.g., reading, lunch, books, chalk, friends, story time, P.E., bus.

2. Ask several students to write their responses on the board; then have other students state a complete sentence, each using one response.

3. Repeat the process with things students don't like; e.g., rest time, bullies, work, lunch, homework.

4 Explain that even though there are both things we like and dislike about school, we still come to school; we come to learn to read, write, count, and one day become leaders as grown ups. We decide to come to school to learn; when we learn we help ourselves.

5. Ask the students if there are other things they do that have both liked and disliked parts to them. Let students identify some of these events (going to the store, watching TV, playing outside, sharing a toy, taking a vacation, doing chores, taking medicine).

6. Ask why students do these things even though each has disliked outcomes or consequences as well as liked. Hopefully, they will say that the positives outweigh the negatives.

Closure:

"Almost everything we do has both liked and disliked outcomes, but we decide to take action when the results outweigh things we do not like."

End this session by having the students recite the model: ***First, Think; Second, Act.***

Mooring Lines:

Baylor, Byrd & Parnell, Peter. *Hawk, I'm Your Brother*. Aladdin. 1986.

Kroll, Steven & Appleby, Ellen. *I'd Like to Be*. Parents. 1987.

Peters, Lauren. *Problems at the North Pole*. Landmark Editions. 1990.

Seuss, Dr. *Hunches and Bunches*. Random House. 1982.

Rosemarie Scotti Hughes, Ph.D. & Pamela C. Kloeppel, Ed.D.

Decision Making
Second Grade Session One

What Can I Do?

Objectives:

Write action sentences

Understand that problems often have more than one solution

Materials:

Paper folded into four quadrants, pencils, chalkboard and chalk, or chart paper and marker.

Procedure:

1. Put a simple math problem on the board, such as 2 + 3 = 5. Explain that even if the numbers are reversed (3 + 2), the answer will still be the same. You may want to illustrate with additional problems.

2. Explain that in real life, there are also many ways to solve a problem. At these times you choose the best way to solve a problem.

3. "Today we are going to talk about choices you we can make when:

    You are *afraid*.

    You are *angry*.

    You are *lonesome*.

    You are *sad*."

4. Write across the board, leaving room to write under each:

    When I am afraid, I can....

    When I am angry, I can....

    When I am lonesome, I can....

    When I am sad, I can....

    Discuss these with the children and write key words under each phrase.

5. Have the children write each partial sentence, one in each quadrant of the paper; then have them complete the sentence either from the lists on the board, or with their own ideas. If there is time, encourage students to draw these four situations on the back of the paper.

6. Ask the students to share their sentences.

Closure:

You can always act, even when you are afraid, angry, lonesome, or sad. You always have a choice of what you can do. First you must think. You must decide what you can/will do: ***First, Think; Second, Act.***

Sailing On:

Be alert for situations of child abuse or neglect. Refer immediately to Child Protection Services if you suspect a harmful situation.

Mooring Lines:

Mayne, William & Benson, Patrick. *The Yellow Book of Hob Stories*. Philome. 1984.

O'Brien, Robert & Bernstein, Zena. *Mrs. Frisby and the Rats of NIMH*. Atheneum. 1971.

Consequences

Objectives:

Practice writing and speaking skills

Understand the definition of "consequence"

Materials:

Book, chalk, dictionary, paper, and pencil.

Procedure:

1. Write the word "CONSEQUENCE" on the board. Ask the students if they know the meaning of the word "consequence." Have them give their own definitions. Drop a book on the floor—the consequence is startled students. Drop a piece of chalk on the floor—the consequence is broken chalk. You may want to discuss some other consequences—what happens if students forget lunch money, sleep too late on a school day, don't do homework, and so forth.

2. Have a student read the definition of *consequence* from an elementary dictionary.

3. Explain that today you are going to tell a story with consequences; they are to find those consequences. They will also be actors in the story you tell.

4. After you read each of the following stories, choose an appropriate number of actors. Then have the students who acted answer the questions, following the story:

   > **Shervonda is new at school. A girl comes up to her and says, "Hi, my name is Donna. I don't think I've seen you at school before." Shervonda feels shy and looks at the floor and walks away.**

   What is the consequence of Shervonda's action? How does Donna feel? What else could Shervonda have done? What could happen then?

   > **Bobby's mom asks him to watch his little brother while she goes shopping. He is working a puzzle with his brother when his friend, Pablo, comes by and asks him to play baseball. Bobby leaves his brother alone to play baseball with Pablo.**

   What is the consequence of Bobby's action? How does his brother feel? How does his mother feel? What happens to Bobby? What else could Bobby do?

Rosemarie Scotti Hughes, Ph.D. & Pamela C. Kloeppel, Ed.D.

Sharon and her friend Lori are at the store. Lori takes a candy bar but does not pay for it. Sharon is afraid and starts to cry.

What are the consequences? What else can Lori do now? What should she have done?

Jamal is out on the playground at school. His friends start picking on a smaller boy. Jamal just stands there.

What are the consequences? How does the small boy feel? How does Jamal feel? What else could Jamal do?

Sam sees his neighbor being shot and the gunman drive away. Sam says nothing.

What are the consequences of this act? What else can Sam do? What are the consequences?

5. Open up discussion to all the students. Do they have any additional ideas or thoughts?

Closure:

"There are consequences and outcomes to any action we take. Even deciding not to act is a decision, with consequences. Is it better to act or do nothing? First think about the consequence then act to get the best result."

Sailing On:

Ask the students to write a sentence about one action they recently took and another sentence about its outcome/consequence. After all are finished have them list one other action they could have decided on instead. What would the consequence have been?

Have the students write the action or decision that was best for them in a complete sentence.

Ask for volunteers to share their papers. One story may take the entire time allotted; this activity can be repeated. Add other scenarios which reflect actions often seen in class.

Mooring Lines:

Davis, Gibbs. *Katy's First Haircut*. Houghton Mifflin. 1985.

Holland, Isabelle. *Kevin's Hat*. Lothrop, Lee & Shephard. 1984.

Mayne, William & Benson, Patrick. *The Yellow Book of Hob Stories*. Philome. 1984.

**Decision Making
Second Grade Session Three**

Rules, Rules, Rules

Objective:

Speak before a group

Understand reasons for rules at home and school

Materials:

Paper, pencils, crayons or markers, chalkboard and chalk, or chart paper and marker.

Procedure:

1. Write on the board in two columns the words "home rules," and "school rules."

2. Ask the children to identify rules they have to follow in school and at home. List these on the board as they are given under the correct heading.

3. After the list is made, pair the students; one writes a rule and the other writes the reason for the rule, both in complete sentences. For example, "Do not talk when you have food in your mouth." "This keeps you from choking on your food."

4. Ask each pair to read the rule and its reason to the class.

5. Have the students discuss these rules, including in their discussion why rules at home and school may be different; e.g., standing in line for lunch at school but not at home.

Closure:

"Rules are made so that we can all live together safely. The more people in one place, the more need to have rules for order. School has more people than home, and has a different purpose, so the rules are different."

Sailing On:

This activity can be used in conjunction with a unit on safety and health. It could also be used to reinforce and emphasize classroom and school rules.

Have students draw a picture of what happens at home or a school when a rule is broken.

Mooring Lines:

Cleary, Beverly. *Ramona and Her Father*. Morrow. 1977.

Hughes, Shirley. *An Evening at Alfie's*. Lothrop, Lee & Shepard. 1984.

Mayne, William & Benson, Patrick. *The Yellow Book of Hob Stories*. Philome. 1984.

Rosemarie Scotti Hughes, Ph.D. & Pamela C. Kloeppel, Ed.D.

**Decision Making
Second Grade Session Four**

The "If" Survey

Objectives:

Use reading and speaking skills in small groups

Practice decision making

Materials:

"If" Survey sheets (page 118), pencils.

Procedure:

1. Explain that today we are going to look at some everyday problems and choose solutions for them.

2. Group the students in fives and have each group read and answer the four questions under one capital letter on the survey sheet. The groups should give reasons for their choices. Remind them to use the *First, Think; Second, Act* model of decision making.

3. When completed, have a reporter from the group read aloud each statement, and discuss why the group made the choice it did.

4. Follow up on each report by asking the consequences of various options taken and not taken.

Closure:

"Every day we make many decisions; we must make them by thinking about the outcome that best meet our needs and treating others fairly. This is not always the first thing that comes into our heads. Good decision making is a skill that must be practiced just like swimming, playing basketball, or riding a bike. The more you practice the better your skill. You practice decision making by using the *First, Think Second, Act* model."

Sailing On:

This lesson can be done individually, rather than in groups of five, if it is better for your class.

After each group report, have entire class vote on all options to see what the majority decided was the best.

Ask each student to write in a complete sentence one decision made today. In a second sentence write the consequence of this decision.

Mooring Lines:

Cleary, Beverly & Porter, George. *Mitch and Amy*. Dell. 1967.

Mayne, William & Benson, Patrick. *The Yellow Book of Hob Stories*. Philome. 1984.

Williams, Vera. *Something Special for Me*. Greenwillow. 1983.

The "If" Survey

A. **If you broke a dish at home, would you**
   Yes No
   - ❏ ❏ 1. Clean it up and not tell anyone?
   - ❏ ❏ 2. Say that someone else did it?
   - ❏ ❏ 3. Tell an adult about it?
   - ❏ ❏ 4. Walk away and pretend that you didn't know about it?

B. **If you made a mistake on a math paper at school, would you**
   Yes No
   - ❏ ❏ 1. Throw away the paper and start over?
   - ❏ ❏ 2. Cry?
   - ❏ ❏ 3. Break your pencil and quit working?
   - ❏ ❏ 4. Correct it and keep on working?

C. **If you were mean to a friend, would you**
   Yes No
   - ❏ ❏ 1. Say nothing and hope that your friend would forget all about it?
   - ❏ ❏ 2. Ask your friend to forgive you?
   - ❏ ❏ 3. Tell your friend why you were mean?
   - ❏ ❏ 4. Tell your friend that someone else made you do it?

D. **If you forgot your pencil, would you**
   Yes No
   - ❏ ❏ 1. Steal one from a classmate?
   - ❏ ❏ 2. Ask to borrow one from a classmate?
   - ❏ ❏ 3. Do without one and fail a test?
   - ❏ ❏ 4. Call your mother for help?

E. **If you saw a crime in your neighborhood, would you**
   Yes No
   - ❏ ❏ 1. Tell your mother?
   - ❏ ❏ 2. Keep quiet?
   - ❏ ❏ 3. Tell a friend?
   - ❏ ❏ 4. Talk to the media?

Rosemarie Scotti Hughes, Ph.D. & Pamela C. Kloeppel, Ed.D.

Decision Making
Second Grade Session Five

Everyday Soaps

Objectives:

Use reading and speaking skills in small and large groups

Practice decision making, identify reasons for decisions, and role play choices with puppets

Materials:

Lunch-size brown bags, construction paper, crayons, glue, paste, tape, scissors, scenes from the bottom of this page, cut out and on cards.

Procedure:

1. Have each student make a paper bag puppet of himself or herself.

2. Next, group students in threes. Explain that one member of each group will read a scene to the class and then the other two will enact the scene with puppets, choosing their own words and actions.

3. After each puppet role play, ask the group to explain the reasons for its decision; ask also for the options they did not use. Why were these options not used?

4. After all puppet scenes have been acted and discussed, have the class recite the model of decision making: ***First, Think; Second, Act.***

Scenes

Closure:

You are taking a spelling test. You don't know how to spell a word and you see the person next to you writing it down.	You leave your lunch ticket or money at home, and you see money on the teacher's desk when the teacher is out of the room.
Your friends tell you to let them in the house to play, but your mother is out, and you are not allowed to let anyone in.	You missed the school bus.
You are told to come right home after school, but a friend asks you to stop by her house.	Someone steals money from you.
A friend asks you if he can borrow your new crayons.	Someone offers to give you drugs.
You see a friend take a pack of gum out of a store without paying for it.	A school bully beats up your best friend, and warns you not to tell.

There is always more than one way to handle a problem. By thinking first of the consequences and outcomes of each way to handle a problem we can make the best decision for ourselves and others. Thinking before we act is always best for us and the people around us.

Sailing On:

You may want to do this in several separate sessions.

Repeat or add scenes of your own so all students have an opportunity to participate.

Mooring Lines:

Gross, Alan. *The I Don't Want to Go to School Book*. Children's Press. 1982.

Moncure, Jane Belk. *John's Choice: A Story About Honesty*. Dandelion House. 1983.

Schwartz, Amy. *Begin at the Beginning*. Harper & Row. 1983.

Waber, Bernard. *Ira Sleeps Over*. Houghton Mifflin. 1972. (Also available as a talking book.)

Rosemarie Scotti Hughes, Ph.D. & Pamela C. Kloeppel, Ed.D.

**Decision Making
Second Grade Session Six**

My Decision

Objectives:

Improve writing and speaking skills

Practice decision making, identifying various options and consequences.

Materials:

Paper and pencil.

Procedure:

1. Have each student write a sentence about a decision he or she must make in the near future. This decision can be one of the child's choosing or selected from the list below:

   To choose a Halloween costume

   To select a Christmas/Hanukkah gift for someone

   To make plans for the summer

   A scout project

   A fun thing to do when Grandmother comes to visit

   To tell or not tell on someone who hurt me

2. On the same paper have students list at least four actions they could take, including doing nothing, and the consequences or outcome of each action.

3. Then have the class discuss their answers. List answers identified by students on the board, in two columns, labeled "acts" and "consequences".

Closure:

Explain each decision to be made sometimes has more than one solution; more than one way of handling it, including doing nothing. "When we do nothing we have also made a decision—to do nothing and accept the outcome that comes. Before we make decisions we must first consider the outcomes of each action. Always remember the *First, Think; Second, Act* method."

Sailing On:

Ask the students to turn in their papers. Review each paper making suggestions for improvement in writing as well as in logic.

Pair the students who have the same decision to be made so they can identify together four actions to be taken and resulting consequences.

Mooring Lines:

Gibbs, Davis. *Katy's First Haircut*. Houghton Mifflin. 1985.

Havill, Juanita. *Jamaica's Find*. Houghton Mifflin. 1986.

Schwartz, Amy. *Begin at the Beginning*. Harper & Row. 1983.

**Decision Making
Third Grade Session One**

Who is Responsible?

Objectives:

Oral discussion

Student understanding of responsibility for decisions

Materials:

Dictionary and "Who is Responsible" sheet (page 123).

Procedure:

1. Write the word "**RESPONSIBLE**" on the board, and ask if anyone knows the meaning of this word.

2. Ask one student to read the definition to the class from an elementary dictionary.

3. Ask the students if they have ever been in a situation where they blamed another person for their trouble, or if someone else unfairly blamed them. Allow time for responses.

4. Tell the children that today we are going to read several situations about students who are having trouble. We decide who is responsible for each situation. Identify one student to read each situation.

5. After each scenario is read, and without discussion, students are to vote by thumbs up or down on who the responsible person is in each.

6. After the voting ask the children to give their reasons for voting for the person they chose.

Closure:

Explain that we, and no one else, are responsible for our own actions. Even though we might have pressure from others to do things and there may be other things we can't control, we are responsible for what we do.

Mooring Lines:

Gaeddert, LouAnn Bigge. *The Kid with Red Suspenders*. E.P. Dutton. 1983.

Smith, Robert Kimmel. *The War with Grandpa*. Delacorte. 1984.

Staunton, Ted. *Taking Care of Crumley*. Kids Can. 1984.

Rosemarie Scotti Hughes, Ph.D. & Pamela C. Kloeppel, Ed.D.

Who is Responsible?

1. John took a comic book from the store and put it in his pocket. The manager caught him. John said that Tyrell told him to do it. Who is responsible? What is responsible behavior for John? _____

2. Roberta punched Shandell. Roberta said she had to do it because Shandell called her a name. Who is responsible? What is responsible behavior for Roberta? _____

3. Aaron took Carlos' pencil. He said he did it because Carlos took his pencil yesterday. Who is responsible? What is responsible behavior for Aaron? _____

4. Hope called the teacher a name in class. She was angry the teacher took away her cassette. Hope had been listening to a tape instead of doing her math. Who is responsible? What is responsible behavior for Hope? _____

5. Gary tripped Tommy because Tommy teased him about his haircut. Who is responsible? What is responsible behavior for Gary? _____

6. Lee broke Shannon's pair of skates. Lee blamed Shannon for having a lousy pair of skates. Who is responsible? What is responsible behavior for Lee? _____

7. Hosea wrote graffiti on the school building after the gang leader told him to do it. Hosea was caught and blamed his graffiti writing on the gang leader. Who is responsible? What is responsible behavior for Hosea? _____

8. Rick stole $10.00 from the teacher. Chris saw him and told the teacher. Rick blamed Chris for getting him in trouble. Who is responsible? What is responsible behavior for Rick? _____

The Gumball Machine

Objectives:

Practice writing and speaking skills

Understand that similar decisions are made for different reasons

Materials:

Handout with gumball machine (page 125) for each student, pencil.

Procedure:

1. Ask the children if anyone ever buys pieces of gum or candy from a coin machine. Discuss the different products and various colors in the machines that they see.

2. Distribute the accompanying handout. Explain that this is a "your-choice" gumball machine. Read the directions on the handout and proceed.

3. Ask the students to write their choices in complete sentences, giving their reason for choices made. An example might be "I chose to see a movie because my mother would take me." These should be written on the back of the handout.

4. Have volunteers share their sentences. After one person has read a sentence, ask if anyone else made the same selection for a different reason. If so, have this student read his sentence.

5. Point out that the decision was the same, but the reason was different—the consequence was the same, but the cause was different.

6. Teach the steps of decision making and put them on the board, using the model that is most appropriate for your class (see introduction, page 93).

Closure:

"Today we each made five decisions, some of our decisions were the same, and some were different. Even though many of our decisions were the same, we often had different reasons for them. Reasons for decisions can be different and individual, just like people are different and individual. The important part of making a decision is following the steps of decision making so we make the best possible choice—a choice that will be good for us and the people we care about."

Mooring Lines:

Hest, Amy. *Maybe Next Year*. Morrow. 1994.

Holland, Isabelle. *Kevin's Hat*. Lothrop, Lee & Shepard. 1984.

Moskin, Marietta Dunston. *Rosie's Birthday Present*. Atheneum. 1981.

Ruthstrom, Dorethea. *The Big Kite Contest*. Pantheon. 1980.

Rosemarie Scotti Hughes, Ph.D. & Pamela C. Kloeppel, Ed.D.

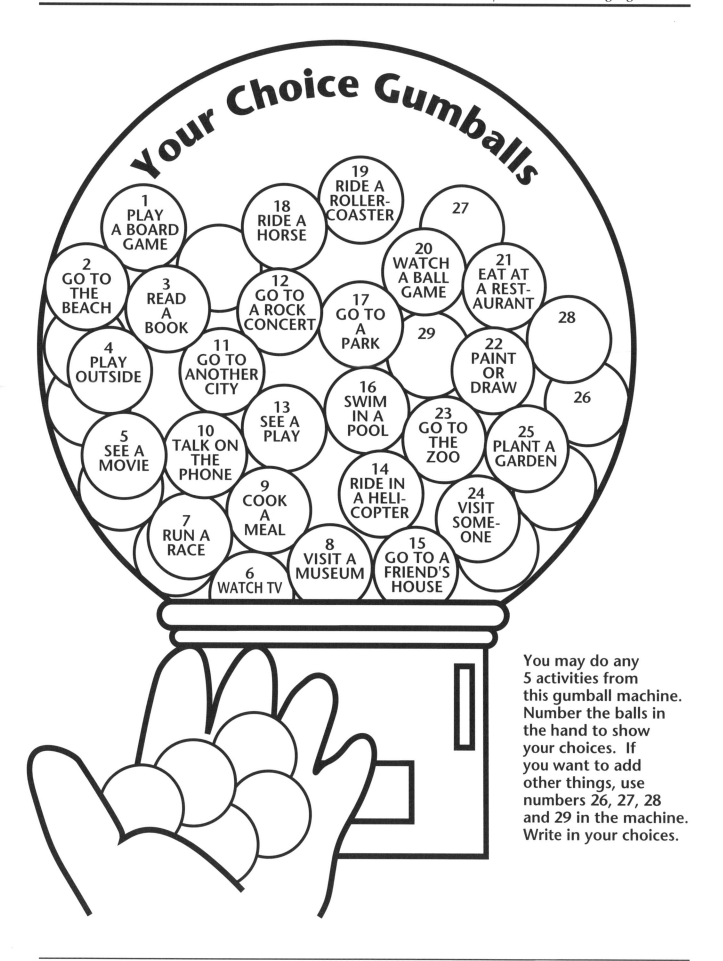

Your Choice Gumballs

1 PLAY A BOARD GAME
2 GO TO THE BEACH
3 READ A BOOK
4 PLAY OUTSIDE
5 SEE A MOVIE
6 WATCH TV
7 RUN A RACE
8 VISIT A MUSEUM
9 COOK A MEAL
10 TALK ON THE PHONE
11 GO TO ANOTHER CITY
12 GO TO A ROCK CONCERT
13 SEE A PLAY
14 RIDE IN A HELICOPTER
15 GO TO A FRIEND'S HOUSE
16 SWIM IN A POOL
17 GO TO A PARK
18 RIDE A HORSE
19 RIDE A ROLLERCOASTER
20 WATCH A BALL GAME
21 EAT AT A RESTAURANT
22 PAINT OR DRAW
23 GO TO THE ZOO
24 VISIT SOMEONE
25 PLANT A GARDEN
26
27
28
29

You may do any 5 activities from this gumball machine. Number the balls in the hand to show your choices. If you want to add other things, use numbers 26, 27, 28 and 29 in the machine. Write in your choices.

Carlos' Choice

Objective:

Practice reading and writing skills

Participate in group decision making and consensus

Materials:

Writing paper, pencils, blackboard and chalk, or chart paper and markers.

Procedure:

1. Divide the children in groups of five and have them choose a recorder who will write on the board.

2. Ask if anyone has had company from out of town. Did anyone receive a present from this visitor? Explain that today we will help someone decide on such a gift.

3. Read the following to the children:

    Carlos is 8 years old. Aunt Juanita is coming to visit and would like to do something special for Carlos. Carlos and his mother sit down and make a list of things that would be special for Carlos. They are: (as you speak, draw a stick figure on the board to represent Carlos; then draw five lines from the figure and a circle at the end of each line. Write the underlined word in each circle.)

    coat—Carlos' winter coat is too small, and when the weather gets colder, he will need a new coat.

    dentist—Carlos has never been to the dentist, and there is a children's clinic opening in the neighborhood.

    bicycle—Carlos has been riding a friend's bicycle and would love to own one. There is a bicycle sale advertised on TV this week.

    tapes and tape player—Carlos enjoys listening to music on the radio but would like to have a tape or CD player and music of his own.

    trip—Carlos has never been to (a popular attraction like Disney World), but has seen ads for it on TV; Carlos would like to go.

4. Each small group must agree on only once choice. To encourage group discussion, ask, "If you were Carlos what would you choose? Why would you choose this? Would it make any difference if you had a toothache? Is there any way Carlos can get more than one of these presents?

Rosemarie Scotti Hughes, Ph.D. & Pamela C. Kloeppel, Ed.D.

5. After the small group discussion, have the reporter from each group write the group's choice and the reason(s) for it on the board.

6. Identify and discuss trends in students' answers; possible trends might be:

> If a coat is selected, a practical decision (warmth) was made; also a coat would last a long time and save his mother money. The coat could also be passed on to Carlos' brother.

> If the dentist is selected, another practical decision was made (Carlos' health). This would also save his mother money.

> If a bicycle is selected, it is also practical (to go places) and would save his mother money. It would also give Carlos some independence and fun.

> If tapes are chosen, the decision is less practical, leaning more to immediate gratification; however, the tape player can be used for a long time and can provide much enjoyment.

> If a trip is chosen, the decision is impractical and is based on "wants, not needs." Additionally, the trip is soon over. However, if Carlos has all other items, a trip is a good decision. It might be a very special time with his aunt. Also Carlos may be very sick and a trip is a last wish.

7. Total the group's votes to determine the class decision.

Closure:

"We make decisions for many different reasons. Sometimes our decisions depend on the weather (if it is cold, we need a coat). Sometimes our health is the reason we make a decision (it is time for a dental check up or we have a toothache). Other times we make decisions because we need or want things. The reason we make decisions change as we change. But good decision making remains the same. It is a step by step process that never changes."

Sailing On:

Assign the students a composition about a similar choice they must make. They are to include all steps of the model of decision making they were taught. Write the story on the board, have the students read it themselves, and make individual decisions, prior to a class discussion.

Have children illustrate their composition.

Mooring Lines:

Carris, Joan Davenport. *When the Boys Ran the House.*

Hest, Amy. *Maybe Next Year.* Morrow. 1994.

Hopkins, Lee Bennett. *Mama & Her Boys.* Harper & Row. 1981.

What Would You Do?

Objectives:

Practice reading and speaking skills

Understand that problems have more than one solution, but not all solutions are good ones

Materials:

Accompanying handout, "What Would You Do?" (page 130), and pencils.

Procedure:

1. Distribute the handout, explaining that each student is to write a complete sentence about what he or she would do in each situation and the reason for this action. There are no right or wrong answers to these questions.

2. When all students have finished, discuss each response, and make a chart on the board tallying students' answers.

   Example:

   #1 Low grade

ask for help	cry
hide paper	ignore
change seat	fuss at teacher
tell mother	do nothing

3. Discuss each response asking for reasons; as reasons are given point out long and short term consequences of each decision.

Closure:

"As we learned today each problem has many solutions. Some solutions help us; some hurt us. Some solutions are easy, but some are difficult. Even doing nothing is a solution, but not always a good solution. Doing nothing often has bad consequences in the future, even if not in the present. So, we must always decide on a solution. We must take charge of consequences that happen to us. We must always act. Doing nothing is having nothing to say about what happens to us. We need to always consider long term consequences as well as immediate wants/needs." Remind the students of the model of decision making from the previous lesson.

 Rosemarie Scotti Hughes, Ph.D. & Pamela C. Kloeppel, Ed.D.

Sailing On:

If this lesson is taught as given, it may take several sessions to complete.

This exercise can also be done in small groups or pairs with each group having only one decision to make. The group would have to write their answer in complete sentences and use a decision-making model. Each group would report to the entire class.

Add other examples that are appropriate for the class and as circumstances arise. You may want to include negative situations which are occurring in class.

Mooring Lines:

Gaeddert, LouAnn Bigge. *The Kid with the Red Suspenders*. E.P. Dutton. Inc. 1983.

Moncure, Jane Belk. *John's Choice: A Story About Honesty*. Dandelion. 1983.

Porte, Barbara Ann. *Harry's Dog*. Greenwillow. 1984.

Steiner, Barbara Annette. *Oliver Dibbs to the Rescue!* Four Winds. 1985.

What Would You Do?

1. You get a low grade on a math test. What would you do? _____

   _____

   Why? _____

   _____

2. You get an "A" on a spelling test. What would you do? _____

   _____

   Why? _____

   _____

3. You mother tells you to wash the dishes, but your favorite TV show is on.

   What would you do? _____

   _____

   Why? _____

   _____

4. Your best friend tells you that he is moving away. What would you do? ____

   _____

   Why? _____

   _____

5. Your little brother calls you a bad name. What would you do? _____

   _____

   Why? _____

   _____

Rosemarie Scotti Hughes, Ph.D. & Pamela C. Kloeppel, Ed.D.

6. You see a schoolmate steal a pencil from a friend. What would you do? ____

_____

Why? _____

_____

7. You see a friend steal money from someone you do not know. What would you do? _____

_____

Why? _____

_____

8. You don't make the team, what would you do?_____

_____

Why? _____

_____

9. You know a classmate has a gun at school. What would you do? _____

_____

Why? _____

_____

10. Your 12 year old brother is drinking beer in his room. What would you do?

_____

Why? _____

_____

11. Someone asks you to be a lookout for the police or store owner while he steals some tapes. What would you do? _____

_____

Why? _____

_____

12. Your father moves away from your home. What would you do? _____

_____

Why? _____

_____

13. You see someone killed. What would you do? _____

_____

Why? _____

_____

14. You receive $25.00 for a gift. What would you do? _____

_____

Why? _____

_____

15. You forgot to get your father a Father's Day gift. What would you do? _____

_____

Why? _____

_____

Rosemarie Scotti Hughes, Ph.D. & Pamela C. Kloeppel, Ed.D.

Decision Making
Third Grade Session Five

Dilemmas

Objectives:

Improve speaking, writing, and vocabulary skills

Understand that problems have more than one solution

Materials:

Elementary dictionary, chalkboard and chalk, paper and pencil, "Dilemmas" sheet (bottom of this page).

Procedure:

1. Ask the students, "Was there ever a time when you were not sure of what to do?" You might tell them of a time in your own experience when you had a dilemma, or ask them to share examples from their lives with the class.

2. Explain that this situation is called a "dilemma." Have a student read the definition of DILEMMA from an elementary dictionary to the class.

3. Pair the students and then write one dilemma on the board from those listed below. Have pairs read the dilemma and brainstorm solutions. Each pair is to choose one appropriate solution, using a decision-making model. Write the steps of the model you choose from page 93 on the board.

Dilemmas:

You are walking home from school and you find a wallet with $25.00 in it.

You are in a shopping mall, and you cannot find your mother.

You order a hamburger and fries at a fast food restaurant, but when you put your hand in your pocket for your money, your money is gone.

You have checked out a book from the school library, but now that it is due, you cannot find it.

Your friend ran away from home.

Your big brother is a gang member.

Your mother doesn't come home all night.

You are beaten up by the school bully.

You win the lottery.

4. As time permits, for each dilemma, select one pair to report to the class, incorporating each step of decision-making in their response.

5. After the pair reports, ask class members for additions, suggestions, or to identify errors in judgment.

6. Have a hand vote for a class decision on the best answer.

Closure:

Explain that dilemmas always have many solutions, but not all solutions are good ones. The more solutions and their consequences we can identify, the better our final decision will be. It will be better because we will consider many outcomes, not act on our first thought; not act with our emotion, but with our brain; not act without considering the consequences to us.

Sailing On:

Assign as homework a paragraph or composition on a dilemma in the student's life. What has the student done to handle it? Why? What other solutions are open? What can happen if another solution is chosen? What circumstances are impacting on the solution?

Be alert to any situation where a child needs to see a school counselor individually, or referred to social services.

Do in two sessions.

Mooring Lines:

Gross, Alan. *The I Don't Want to Go to School Book.* Children's. 1982.

Prelutsky, Jack. *Be Glad Your Nose is on Your Face.* Greenwillow. 1984.

Seuss, Dr. *Hunches and Bunches.* Random House. 1982.

Rosemarie Scotti Hughes, Ph.D. & Pamela C. Kloeppel, Ed.D.

Decision Making
Third Grade Session Six
Who Makes Decisions for Me?

Objectives:

Creative writing

Understand that we make many of our own decisions

Materials:

Handout for each student, "Who Makes Decisions for Me" (page 136), and pencils.

Procedure:

1. Tell the students that all of us make some of our own decisions, but many times other people (parents, teachers, employers) make decisions for us.

2. Tell the students that today they will complete a chart about who makes decisions for them.

3. Distribute the chart and explain directions.

4. After students complete and tally their chart have them discuss their answers in class.

5. At the end of the discussion emphasize that even though other people make decisions for us, we also make many of our own.

Closure:

"Even though you are young, you make more decisions of your own than others make for you. You, therefore, have a great deal of control for your own behavior; how you choose to act, react, or not to act is in your own hands; you can't blame others for your own choices. You reap the rewards for good choices and suffer the problems resulting from bad choices."

Sailing On:

Assign creative writing about one decision in student's life which someone else controls, but the student would like to control. What would be done differently if the student had control? Why? What would the consequences be? Tell students to use the decision-making model you have been teaching in determining their response.

Mooring Lines:

Greene, Constance Clarke. *Alexandra the Great*. Viking. 1982.

Holl, Kristi Diane. *Footsteps Up My Back*. Atheneum. 1984.

Prelutsky, Jack. *My Mother Says I'm Sickening*. Greenwillow. 1984.

Taking Responsibility. Tom Snyder Productions. 1988. (Microcomputer Program).

Who Makes Decisions for Me?

NAME: _____

Place a check mark in each box that applies to you.

Me	Parent	Teacher	Others	
❏	❏	❏	❏	Food I eat at home
❏	❏	❏	❏	Food I eat away from home
❏	❏	❏	❏	Clothes I wear
❏	❏	❏	❏	TV shows I watch
❏	❏	❏	❏	Movies I see
❏	❏	❏	❏	Grades I get
❏	❏	❏	❏	How I treat classmates
❏	❏	❏	❏	Books I read
❏	❏	❏	❏	Fights I have
❏	❏	❏	❏	Homework I do
❏	❏	❏	❏	When I brush my teeth
❏	❏	❏	❏	Baths/showers I take
❏	❏	❏	❏	Where I go on trips
❏	❏	❏	❏	Haircuts I have
❏	❏	❏	❏	Shoplifting I do
❏	❏	❏	❏	Drugs I take
❏	❏	❏	❏	Friends I have
❏	❏	❏	❏	Church I attend
❏	❏	❏	❏	Games I play
❏	❏	❏	❏	People I love
❏	❏	❏	❏	School rules I obey

____   ____   ____   ____   TOTALS

Rosemarie Scotti Hughes, Ph.D. & Pamela C. Kloeppel, Ed.D.

Decision Making
Fourth Grade Session One

Mother is Making Me

Objectives:

Composition writing

Practice decision making skills

Materials:

Paper and pencil for each student.

Procedure:

1. Ask the students, "Do your parents have goals for you?" Goals can range from making good grades to playing little league ball, from being in the school band to making the cheering squad. We often feel pressure from our parents to do more than we are doing.

2. Ask the students to give one of their own goals.

3. Then ask, "Why do parents have goals for us that are different than our own goals?" Write reasons given on the board. Be certain to include on the board that parents can see longer term consequences/outcomes than children.

4. Explain that older people—parents—can often see more outcomes/ consequences to actions than younger people because they have lived through these consequences. Because they have experienced these consequences, they can help us with the steps of decision making.

5. Have the children write a paper on a goal their parent has for them that they do not share or are having a hard time meeting. In this paper they are to give their parent's reasons, their own reasons, any solutions they see, and actions necessary to create this solution. They are to follow a decision-making model.

Closure:

"Many times in our lives, parents will have goals for us we do not share. We must always ask why. Are these goals good for us or bad for us? Are they good for us in the future or right now? If we help Dad in the garage now, will we be better able to do things, at home, as an adult? If we study now, will we get good grades? Good grades are important to our future, but studying means we can't always play or watch our favorite TV show. Which is more important to us? Is it the TV show we will soon forget or see during summer reruns, or good grades? How will piano lessons help us in the future? Can they open doors to a career or college scholarship? Always think long term—not short term. Deciding will help us see things long term, not just for today."

Mooring Lines:

Mills, Claudia. *The Secret Carousel.* Four Winds. 1983.

Rodowsky, Colby F. *Hi. My Name is Henley.* Farrar, Straus & Giroux. 1982.

Ruckman, Ivy. *What's an Average Kid Like Me Doing Way Up Here?* Delacorte. 1983.

Viorst, Judith. *Fifteen, Maybe Sixteen, Things to Worry About.* MacMillan. 1981.

Looking Over All the Choices

Objectives:

Practice speaking and writing skills

Participate in group and individual decision making

Materials:

Scenarios, cut from the handout, "Looking Over All the Choices" (page 139), and taped onto index cards, pencils.

Procedure:

1. Divide the class into groups of three and give each an index card with a scenario from "Looking Over All the Choices" on it.

2. Explain that when students are working on a subject such as math, there is usually only one correct answer to a problem. When there is a spelling test, there is generally one correct way to spell a word. However, as we go about our daily lives, there is often more than one way to solve a personal problem. On each index card is a problem that can be solved in more than one way.

3. Have each group discuss its given situation and report to the class how it solved the problem. Remind groups to use a decision-making model in their solution and class report. (See introduction, page 93).

Closure:

Lives are made up of constant problems to solve; each decision about one problem moves us towards other problems and other decisions we must tackle. Often we can never go back after a decision has been made or an act is completed. Therefore we must make decisions that are well thought out, that have solutions which help us or someone we love.

Sailing On:

Assign as homework or classwork a creative writing on a personal problem to be solved, using the *D.E.C.I.D.E./S.A.I.L./D.O.G.* method.

The next day ask for volunteers to discuss their problem and solution to it in class. After each student's presentation, ask if others had the same problem but solved it differently. What happened?

Mooring Lines:

Diggs, Lucy. *Everyday Friends*. Atheneum. 1986.

Frost, Robert. *The Road Not Taken,* a poem.

Hest, Amy. *Maybe Next Year*. Clarion. 1982.

Viorst, Judith. *If I Were in Charge of the World*. MacMillan. 1981.

Looking Over All the Choices

Your last two clean socks do not match.

You get to school, and someone tells you that there is a rip in the seam of your clothes.

You are at a friend's house for dinner, and his mother serves meatloaf, which you hate.

Someone offers you a beer.

Someone stole something from you, and you think you know who did it.

Some students at school have drugs and offer them to you.

You left your key on the kitchen table, and now you are locked out of your apartment.

You hear that your best friend has told a lie about you.

You are around an adult who likes to hug you, but it makes you feel uncomfortable.

You see someone who is bigger than you steal a classmate's wallet.

A new student is better than you in physical education class.

Your mother tells you that the family will soon move to another neighborhood.

You want to buy a gift for someone, but you don't have enough money.

You did not study for the test.

You hurt someone's feelings.

I Am...

Objectives:

Use adjectives as personal descriptors in a composition

Identify reasons for and logical consequences of decisions

Materials:

A mirror, blackboard and chalk, elementary dictionary, paper and pencil.

Procedure:

1. Have the students take turns looking into a mirror. Ask them to describe what they see. Most will describe their physical appearance.

2. Next, ask the students to identify personal characteristics they can't see. Write these characteristics on the board.

3. Have each child choose three words from the above list that best describe himself or herself; these words are to be written at the top of the paper, I AM _____, _____, and _____.

   Some suggestions for characteristics are: wise, beautiful, healthy, happy, kind, generous, funny, helpful, brave, strong, honest, caring, neat, curious, thrifty, friendly, smart, sharing, loving, athletic, responsible, dependable, studious, and cheerful.

4. Explain that these descriptive words are called adjectives.

Closure:

"Today we shared personal characteristics and a time when we used/exhibited these characteristics. Such descriptive characteristics are called adjectives. Adjectives are logical consequences of the actions we take or do not take. People decide what we and others are like based on our/their actions. Then they use adjectives to describe us and others. They make logical decisions based on what they see or hear. We must remember this when we act. We must decide what we do based on the outcome/consequence of our actions. One of the outcomes/consequences of each action is what people think of us. We must always remember to make the best decision for ourselves or someone we love. We make good decisions by using a decision-making model." Have the students recite the model you choose to teach: ***D.E.C.I.D.E./S.A.I.L./D.O.G.***

Rosemarie Scotti Hughes, Ph.D. & Pamela C. Kloeppel, Ed.D.

Sailing On:

Each student is to write a dictionary definition of the three adjectives selected. Ask each child to tell about a time when he or she exhibited one of these characteristics. What was the situation? What happened? Why? What were the consequences? How was life different afterwards? What else could have been done? Why wasn't it?

Have students discuss their writing in class before submitting to their portfolio.

Once students select their personal adjectives, have them read a book and write a book report about a person with these same characteristics. Have students compare their own personal characteristics with those of the main character. Work with the librarian in advance so he or she is prepared to supply the books.

Mooring Lines:

Blaine, Marge & Wallner, John. *The Terrible Thing That Happened at our House*. Parents Magazine. 1975.

Brooke, William. *A Telling of the Tales: Five Stories*. HarperCollins. 1990.

It's Your Vacation

Objectives:

Complete a research project and make an oral report

Understand a final decision may require many intermediate decisions

Materials:

Sheet,, "Vacation Decisions" (page 143), pencil.

Procedure:

1. Pair students or put them in groups of four; explain that they are best friends and have been given the responsibility of planning a vacation. You will make all the decisions necessary. You may plan on spending $_____ (whatever amount is appropriate for your class).

2. Discuss decisions which must be made. List these on the board.

   Where? (warm, cold, theme park, city, country)

   Transportation to/from

   Place to stay (hotel, campground, relative's home)

   Places to eat

   Things to do there

   Clothes to take

   Things to buy (bathing suit, film and camera, etc.)

3. Each group is to make and report its vacation plans to the class.

4. After all reports are completed discuss common themes and any omissions.

5. Distribute "Vacation Decisions" sheets to each pair and explain they are now to research their vacation site. Students are to complete one sheet for each place under consideration.

6. Give students up to a week to complete their research, providing them with suggestions for research, e.g., library, AAA, travel agents, 800 phone numbers for hotels and transportation. Ask the students to share additional research sources they find.

7. On the due date, groups are to review their vacation plans and identify each step of their decision making process using the D.E.C.I.D.E./S.A.I.L./D.O.G. decision-making model.

Closure:

Explain that planning must be done and decisions must be made before anything can be successful, e.g., a vacation trip, good grades, a week's groceries, and so forth. The steps of making good decisions are the same, regardless of decisions to be made.

Sailing On:

Each group is to now develop a description of the place to be visited- something that would encourage others to visit the place chosen. Students can include slogans, jingles, pictures. Attached to this creative writing is to be a copy of the appropriate "Vacation Decision" research.

Invite a speaker who is knowledgeable about a vacation site selected or the travel industry to discuss these sites.

Mooring Lines:

Use the same procedure to plan a class trip or class project.

Assign readings about places selected, e.g., geographical, historical.

Alcock, Vivian. *Travelers by Night*. Dell. 1990.

Bawden, Nina. *Henry*. Dell. 1990.

Bawden, Nina. *The Finding*. Lothrop, Lee & Shepard. 1985.

Beirne, Barbara. *Under the Lights: A Child Model at Work*. Carolrhoda. 1988.

Brooke, William. *A Telling of the Tales: Five Stories*. HarperCollins. 1990.

Vacation Decisions

PLACE _____

TRANSPORTATION	$_____	$_____	$_____	$_____
	Air	Bus	Car	Train
LIVING ARRANGEMENTS	$_____	$_____	$_____	
	Hotel	Camp	Relative's Home	
FOOD COST PER DAY	$_____			
THINGS TO DO	_____	_____	_____	
COST	$_____	$_____	$_____	
CLOTHES TO TAKE	_____	_____	_____	
	_____	_____	_____	
THINGS TO BUY	_____	_____	_____	
	_____	_____	_____	
WHO WILL GO?	_____	_____	_____	
	_____	_____	_____	

Making Friends

Objectives:

Improve speaking and writing skills

Application of decision making to school situations

Materials:

None

Procedure:

1. Ask the children to think about a time when they had a hard time making friends or a time that they felt uncomfortable around people they did not know. If appropriate, remind them that next year they will be attending a middle school and will make many new friends. Ask them if they feel confident about making new friends or if it is a little scary for them. Let students respond.

2. Tell them that today they are going to hear a story about a girl who is not sure how to make new friends and they will have an opportunity to help her. The story is written below:

> Michelle is a rather quiet girl, who is now in the sixth grade. She seldom talks to anyone. After dinner, she usually goes to her room to read or listen to music. She spends a lot of time by herself. Her mother is concerned about her and suggests she ask some friends over to spend the night. Michelle said that she didn't really know anyone to ask.
>
> Michelle's mother wanted her to try out for the school chorus, but Michelle was afraid she wouldn't be good enough and didn't think the students in the chorus would want her, anyway. She is very lonely and feels sorry for herself.
>
> Michelle would like to go to the movies and to parties with friends but doesn't know how to go about finding friends.
>
> Middle school is so big! She is so new there! Everyone seems to have a group of friends already. Some groups of girls are loud and noisy. Others skip school, now and then; another crowd of girls all have boyfriends. There are some students who seem to get all "A's," and others are popular with everyone. How can Michelle find a group of friends?

Rosemarie Scotti Hughes, Ph.D. & Pamela C. Kloeppel, Ed.D.

3. Ask the students to write about solutions to Michelle's problem.

> What kind of person do people like for a friend?
>
> How can Michelle change to be this type of person?
>
> How can Michelle find people of similar interests?
>
> What kind of friends are good to have?
>
> What kind of friends would not be good to have?
>
> Do friendships develop right after you meet people? Why? Why not?
>
> What is the first step Michelle should take?
>
> What have you done to make friends in the past?
>
> What will you do when you go to middle school?

4. Collect and read papers; edit writing skills and note concerns. Include this paper in student's portfolio.

Closure:

Middle school can be somewhat scary since it is a new place—a different and larger world. All new sixth graders will be nervous the first few days of school. But middle school is also a great opportunity to use our decision making skills. We will decide how to handle friends; we will decide how hard we want to work; we will decide how well we want to behave. Then as now, it is our decision. Our future is in our own hands.

Sailing On:

Ask the students to write a paper on their biggest concern about attending middle school. What options do they have to handle this concern. Follow a decision-making model in determining a plan of action (See introduction, page 93).

Mooring Lines:

Gaskin, Carol & Price, Alexander. *The Master of Mazes*. Troll. 1985

Terris, Susan. *The Latchkey Kids*. Farrar, Straus & Giroux. 1986.

Wordfind

Objectives:

Build a decision making vocabulary

Understand the value of responsible decision making

Materials:

Accompanying "Wordfind" handout (page 147), class dictionary, blackboard and chalk, or chartpaper and marker.

Procedure:

1. Explain that today we are going to "brainstorm." If the students are not familiar with the term, tell them that saying anything which comes into their brain about the topic is brainstorming.

2. Ask the students to brainstorm words or ideas about "making decisions." Write these words on the board.

3. Have the students discuss these words, giving examples of decisions they have made.

4. Next, distribute "Wordfind," and have the students find words about decision making; this can be done in pairs or completed individually by students.

5. Review all words as a class and explain the meaning of words with which the class is not familiar. Also have a student read the definition of these unfamiliar words from a class dictionary. After each definition is read, have another student use the word in a sentence.

Closure:

Explain that the English language has many words which describe the decision making process—even some not in Wordfind but in our decision making procedure. Review the steps of decision-making by having students recite one model.

Ask the students to identify words from a model that are not in "Wordfind". Explain that there are still others. Ask the students to identify any other words they know. Such a large number of words about decisions show the importance of decision making in our lives. Unless our decisions are well thought out, they are not responsible decisions and cause us to lose control of our actions.

Sailing On:

Have the students create their own word find with words from brainstorming session.

Mooring Lines:

Gaskin, Carol & Price, Alexander. *The Forbidden Towers*. Troll. 1985.

Rosemarie Scotti Hughes, Ph.D. & Pamela C. Kloeppel, Ed.D.

Word Find

```
D  E  C  I  D  E  A  Z  X  J  U  D  G  E  Y
E  B  H  G  X  V  K  N  I  H  T  E  A  P  M
T  S  O  Q  H  T  P  S  D  E  U  D  T  Z  A
E  I  O  V  C  M  I  E  I  U  O  U  H  L  K
R  A  S  E  L  E  C  T  L  D  D  C  E  M  E
M  G  E  R  A  F  K  T  E  W  N  E  R  I  S
I  N  E  D  Q  J  L  L  M  E  I  I  S  G  U
N  P  U  I  G  K  E  E  M  Y  F  I  X  Y  R
E  L  E  C  T  S  L  U  A  N  K  S  U  W  E
F  A  L  T  R  I  U  Q  O  P  T  I  O  N  F
K  N  O  W  S  J  R  C  O  N  C  L  U  D  E
```

CHOOSE	ELECT	PICK
CONCLUDE	FIND OUT	PLAN
CONFIRM	FIX	RULE
DECIDE	JUDGE	SELECT
DEDUCE	KNOW	SETTLE
DETERMINE	MAKE SURE	THINK
DILEMMA	OPTION	VERDICT

```
D E C I D E A Z X J U D G E Y
E B H G X V K N I H T E A P M
T S O Q H T P S D E U D T Z A
E I O V C M I E I U O U H L K
R A S E L E C T L D D C E M E
M G E R A F K T E W N E R I S
I N E D Q J L L M E I I S G U
N P U I G K E M Y F I X Y Y R
E L E C T S L U A N K S U W E
F A L T R I U Q O P T I O N F
K N O W S J R C O N C L U D E
```

CHOOSE	ELECT	PICK
CONCLUDE	FIND OUT	PLAN
CONFIRM	FIX	RULE
DECIDE	JUDGE	SELECT
DEDUCE	KNOW	SETTLE
DETERMINE	MAKE SURE	THINK
DILEMMA	OPTION	VERDICT

Rosemarie Scotti Hughes, Ph.D. & Pamela C. Kloeppel, Ed.D.

Decision Making
Fifth Grade Session Three

Sensible Solutions

Objectives:

Improve reading skills

Consensus-building in decision making

Materials:

Accompanying "Sensible Solutions" handout (page 150), pencils, decision model handout.

Procedure:

1. Pair students and explain that they are going to help each other solve problems.

2. Distribute a handout to each pair of students; the students are to read "Sensible Solutions" and use a decision-making model to identify solutions possible for each situation, then determine the best solution for each situation.

3. Give each student a copy of the model you choose: **D.E.C.I.D.E./ S.A.I.L./D.O.G.** (See page 93.)

4. Select one pair to report on one situation. The report must be given using the decision model selected.

5. Ask the class to discuss this report and their agreement or disagreement with the best solution.

6. Repeat with all situations on the handout.

Closure:

"When we use a decision-making model, we make better decisions because we think about all possible solutions and the consequence of each solution. We consider what will happen before we act. Is this action good for us right now? In the future? Based on the consequences and outcomes we have identified, we make the best decision we can. Only by thinking before we act, can we make good decisions."

Mooring Lines:

Hall, Lynn. *The Leaving.* Charles Scribner's Sons. 1980.

Lepstyle, Robert. *The Contender.* HarperCollins. 1967.

Mathis, Sharon Bell. *Sidewalk Story.* Viking Penguin. 1986.

Sensible Solutions

A. Ann Davis must travel from (two cities in your state) and back on the same day to attend a business meeting. She does not want to spend more than $40 on the trip. Should she:

1. Go by hot-air balloon.
2. Take a train.
3. Go by plane.
4. Ride a horse.
5. Drive her car.
6. Row a boat up the river.
7. Ride a motorcycle.
8. Hitchhike.
9. Take a bus.
10. Ride a bicycle.

B. Charlie is a fifth grader. What should he do next Saturday to help his family? He is allergic to grasses and weeds.

1. Do his homework.
2. Clean his room.
3. Mow the lawn.
4. Baby-sit little brother.
5. Wash windows.
6. Pull the weeds in the yard.
7. Polish everyone's shoes.
8. Fix his skates.
9. Go to the movies.
10. Wash dad's car.

C. Mike lives with his mother and two sisters. His mother has a part-time job, but it seems as though there is never quite enough money for all of the things that they need. Mike has $25 he has been saving. His aunt and uncle gave him $50 for a birthday present. What should Mike to with the money.

1. Buy a new tape player.
2. Buy a savings bond.
3. Buy a gold chain for himself.
4. Buy a bicycle.
5. Go to a theme park
6. Take some friends out.
7. Give his mom some money.
8. Save money for Christmas presents for his family.
9. Put the money in a bank
10. Buy his own jacket.

D. What should Kim do if she is not feeling well?

1. Ask for some medicine.
2. Go to sleep.
3. Tell an adult.
4. Pretend she's O.K.
5. See a doctor.
6. Get a new haircut.
7. Take a friend's medicine.
8. Go out to play.
9. Fix some hot soup.
10. Stay home from school.

E. Tony has not done his homework. What should he do?

1. Stay home from school.
2. Do his homework on the bus.
3. Copy Sally's homework.
4. Tell the teacher that he hasn't done it.
5. Forge a note from his mother saying he was sick last night.
6. Go to the clinic.
7. Take someone else's homework.
8. Volunteer to stay after school and make it up.
9. Tell the teacher that his little brother ripped it.
10. Decide to do the homework next time.

 Rosemarie Scotti Hughes, Ph.D. & Pamela C. Kloeppel, Ed.D.

Decision Making
Fifth Grade Session Four

Tough Decisions

Objectives:

Improve speaking, reading and writing skills

Learn degrees of difficulty in decision-making

Materials:

Accompanying handout, "Tough Decisions" (page 153), pencils.

Procedure:

1. Identify with students some decisions they often make. Ask, as each example is given, if the decision is difficult or easy to make. Use the decisions below to generate discussion as necessary:

   If someone asks you to a sleep over is it hard or easy to decide to go?

   If you have a choice of a new sweater or new shoes, is it a hard or easy decision to make?

   If you can choose to stay after school for detention or sweep the floors after lunch, is it hard or easy to decide which to do?

   If a friend wants to talk on the phone and you have homework to do, can you make a decision quickly about what to do?

2. Explain that, "Today, we are going to take a survey to see which decisions are hard for us to make and which are easy."

3. Distribute "Tough Decision" handout, and tell students to circle the number of the appropriate response, 1, 2, or 3.

4. When everyone is finished, take a count of the number of 1 (easy), 2 (medium), and 3 (hard) answers for the first question. Repeat the process for each question. Discuss those questions that had the most diverse answers.

Closure:

"Decisions can be easy or hard. Some decisions are relatively easy, i.e., deciding on a television show to watch. Others are difficult, i.e., deciding on what to do when a friend breaks the law or a future career. All our lives we will have both easy and hard decisions to make. Whatever type of decision it is, it will be better if we use a decision-making model before we act."

Sailing On:

Discuss each "Tough Decisions" question using a decision-making model, i.e., ***D.E.C.I.D.E./S.A.I.L./D.O.G.*** (See page 93.)

As classwork or homework assign a paper entitled "The Hardest Decision I Ever Had to Make." In this paper students are to identify the decision they made, what happened, why, and how they would handle the same decision today. Would the outcome be different using one of the models of decision making?

When reviewing assignments be sensitive to situations that may need to be discussed individually with the student or referred to the counselor.

Mooring Lines:

Bauer, Marion Dane. *On My Honor*. Houghton/Clarion. 1986.

Beatty, Patricia. *Skedaddle, Charley*. Morrow. 1987.

Bierhorst, John. *The Naked Bear: Folktales of the Iroquois*. Morrow. 1987.

Blaine, Marge & Wallner, John. *The Terrible Thing that Happened at Our House*. Parents Magazine. 1975.

Blume, Judy. *Just as Long as We're Together*. Dell. 1988.

Kaufman, Charles. *The Frog and the Beanpole*. Lothrop, Lee & Shepard. 1980.

Lowry, Lois. *Anastasia At Your Service*. Houghton, 1982.

Nathanson, Laura. *The Trouble with Wednesdays*. Bantam. 1987.

Ruby, Lois. *Pig-out Inn*. Houghton. 1987.

Tough Decisions

Easy	Medium	Hard	
1	2	3	1. You have a test to take tomorrow, but you want to watch a movie on TV.
1	2	3	2. You find a wallet with $100 and a driver's license in it.
1	2	3	3. Your cousin tells you he stole a sweater from a store.
1	2	3	4. You see someone write an obscene word on the bathroom wall in school; later, the principal asks you if you know who did it.
1	2	3	5. You can have as a gift a new coat or a tape player with headphones.
1	2	3	6. You need to go to summer school, but your grandmother has asked you to vacation with her.
1	2	3	7. You know who cheated on the test and he is your best friend.
1	2	3	8. You can choose to attend camp this summer or stay home and earn money by cutting the neighbors' grass. You won't be hired unless you agree to be there all summer.
1	2	3	9. You have $5.00 to go to the movies, but your mother is sick and flowers would cheer her up.
1	2	3	10. You have been offered drugs by one of the "cool" older boys. Will you or won't you?

Look at the numbers that you circled. Do you have mostly ones, twos, or threes?

If you circled #1 most often, you make decisions very quickly. You may know yourself very well and know what to do in most situations.

If you circled #3 most often, you may not be sure of what to do in most situations. Discussing these situations with others and following the *D.E.C.I.D.E./S.A.I.L./D.O.G.* method will provide you with help in making decisions.

If you circled #2 most often, or had a mix of one, two, and three, you are in the middle—in some areas you know just what you would do, and in others you need to work on your decision-making skills. Always remember the *D.E.C.I.D.E./S.A.I.L.* method of decision making.

What Can You Do?

Objectives:

Improve speaking skills through discussion and role play situations.
Practice individual and group decision making.

Materials:

Dictionary.

Procedure:

1. Explain to the children that every day, when we are with others, we make decisions about how to act. We may not even be aware we are making these decisions. We may have automatic ways of acting at such times; automatic ways we have used so often that they have become habits. But we can respond differently. We can make decisions to act differently.

2. Today we will discuss situations which occur between children our ages; then we will role play solutions to these situations. Each situation requires a decision be made.

3. First asks students to define the words "habit" and "role play;" then have a student read their dictionary definitions.

4. Role play situations are listed under "What Can You Do?" Since each situation can have more than one solution, give several children an opportunity to role play the same situation. Select children carefully so that different solutions/decisions will be portrayed. After each situation has been role played by several students, ask the participants to discuss their thinking and feelings. Then have the class vote on the solution they believe to be the best.

Closure:

"We can always change the way we act by deciding to act differently—by thinking before we do—by using a decision-making model. It is very hard to change a behavior; sometimes it takes weeks of trying. The experts say it takes at least six weeks of hard work to change a habit. Behavior towards others is a habit. It too can be changed by hard work and thinking before we act."

Sailing On:

Use additional situations which have been creating problems in the classroom.

Assign creative writing about a habit which the student wants/needs to change. What can he do? What will he do? How can a decision-making model help?

Rosemarie Scotti Hughes, Ph.D. & Pamela C. Kloeppel, Ed.D.

Mooring Lines:

Alexander, Lloyd. *The Illyrian Adventure.* Dell. 1987.

Alcock, Vivian. *The Monster Garden.* Dell. 1990.

Barrie, Barbara. *Lone Star.* Delacorte. 1990.

Bauer, Marion Dane. *On My Honor.* Houghton/Clarion. 1986.

Bierhorst, John. *The Naked Bear: Folktales of the Iroquois.* Morrow. 1987.

Bowden, Nina. *The Outside Child.* Lothrop, Lee & Shepard. 1989.

Dutton, Cheryl & Smith, Wendy. *Not in Here Dad!* Children's Press. 1989.

Jackson, Alison & Hearn, Diane Dawson. *Crane's Rebound.* Dutton Children's Books. 1991.

What Can You Do?

You said some mean things about Tamika to the other children, and now Tamika feels hurt. You sit beside her on the bus on the way home. What will you do?

You are with a group of middle school students who begin teasing your classmate; he is small in size. What do you do?

Maria's father was arrested and put in jail. She feels embarrassed, and doesn't want to be in school. You are walking down the hall with her. What do you do?

Greg is very shy. He does not like to speak in class. One day he gives a wrong answer to a question, and some people laugh at him. You are sitting next to him at lunch. What do you do?

Your father has asked you to befriend a new neighbor and show him around the school in September. He has a disability and has difficulty walking. What would you do?

Your mother and your best friend's mother have had a big argument. How will you treat your best friend?

Decision Making
Fifth Grade Session Six

I'd Rather Be...."

Objectives:

Non-verbal decision-making

Understand that a career selection requires several decisions

Materials:

Dictionary.

Procedure:

1. Arrange the room so that two walls are clear of furniture.

2. Explain to the students that they are going to make a choice. They will not tell you their choice, but will walk to a certain place in the room showing their decision. Indicate clearly where the students are to walk in response to each question.

3. Read each choice slowly and make sure all words are understood. Give plenty of time between each statement so students do not feel rushed in decision making.

    Would you rather:

    Eat hamburgers or hot dogs?

    Have a banana split or an ice cream cone?

    Have winter or summer?

    Listen to rap or jazz?

    Go to the library or the movies?

    Play the piano or drums?

    Spend the night with a friend or stay home?

    Read a story or a poem?

    Have jewelry made of silver or gold?

    Be a singer or a dancer?

    Vacation on a mountain or at the ocean?

    Ride a bus or an airplane?

    Be an elephant or a giraffe?

4. Observe the children carefully as they walk. Do some make decisions quickly, and others take more time? Are there some items that divide the class 50-50? Do girls decide one way and boys another? Are the majority of the students on one side and only a few on the other? Is there a religious or racial difference? Is peer influence evident?

5. As each choice is made, stop and discuss it before going on to the next choice. Ask reasons choices are made. Was it hard to decide? Why? Were they influenced by others? By whom?

Rosemarie Scotti Hughes, Ph.D. & Pamela C. Kloeppel, Ed.D.

6. After all choices are made, explain that the choices just made were fairly simple choices, but they still thought about them before they acted. They thought before they moved. Some other choices in life are more difficult, choices which have a long term effect on our lives. One such choice is a career choice. Then have a student read the definition of a "career" choice from a dictionary.

7. Have the students give their own career goals. What decisions can they make now that will help them reach their goals?

Closure:

Choices you make about school now will influence what you will do as an adult. Every career requires learning in grade school, middle school and high school. Most require training after high school, either in college or technical school. The military is also an option for many people. The good study habits you set now will be used all your lives.

Sailing On:

Have students complete creative writing assignment on what they want to be when they grow up (their career choice or choices), and why they made this choice or choices. Have them include the steps/actions they must take, beginning in the fifth grade to obtain this goal. What do they have to do in middle school, high school, college? What community experiences are required for this goal?

After reviewing papers for writing skills, note on papers decisions and actions that are omitted by student, i.e., good grades, certain courses, hard work, high school athletics, NCAA core courses requirements.

Invite a college coach to speak with students about what it takes to earn an athletic scholarship, including good grades in academic courses while in high school.

Mooring Lines:

Bauer, Marion Dane. *On My Honor.* Houghton/Clarion. 1986.

Clifford, Elthel Rosenberg. *The Rocking Chair Rebellion.* Houghton Mifflin. 1978.

Lipstyle, Robert. *The Contender.* HarperCollins. 1967.

McAllister, Marcia & Lazzarino, Luciano. *Steven Spielberg, He Makes Great Movies.* Rourke Enterprises. 1989.

Notes:

Rosemarie Scotti Hughes, Ph.D. & Pamela C. Kloeppel, Ed.D.

Peer Relationships

Introduction

The goal of any school system is to produce graduates able to take their places in society, contributing their own unique talents and gifts for the greater good. To become a productive member of society, an individual needs:

— a sense of belonging

— a feeling of worth

— opportunities to interact with others

— opportunities to give of oneself to others

— opportunities to use individual skills and talents

— experiences of closeness and caring.

Children in our society need to feel wanted and of value. Children need to learn how to value each other. There are far too many elements in society that victimize children—divorce, drugs, violence, child pornography, and abuse.

Children may often follow negative role models to gain acceptance. Younger and younger children are becoming involved in selling drugs and killing and wounding others. They feel accepted by gangs that fill their need to belong, yet are unable to discern that they are being used for harmful purposes.

Fostering respect for each other in the classroom, teaching responsible behavior in school and elsewhere, and assessing attitudes and behaviors are components that build positive peer relationships. These components are in this peer relationship curriculum.

I Am Friendly

Objectives:

Developing language patterns through oral communication

Understanding characteristics of a friend

Materials:

Badges, printed on following page, tape or pins for badges.

Procedure:

1. Explain that today we will talk about being friends. Ask the children to think about a special friend. "How do you know this person is your friend?" Allow ample time for answers.

2. Next ask, "What do you do to let others know that you are a friend?"

3. After this question has been answered by several children, ask them to name their school friends. Be sure to include the principal, bus driver, custodian, cafeteria staff, school counselor, nurse, and you, the teacher.

4. Distribute badges for students to wear. Explain that today is "Special Friend Day" for the class. Have each child print his or her name on the badge, or have these ready for the children.

5. Brainstorm with the children how they can do one special thing today to show others that they can be friends.

Closure:

End with a go-round (giving each child the opportunity to answer), with each child completing the sentence, "Today I will be a friend by...."

Mooring Lines:

Asch, Frank. *Bear's Bargain.* Prentice-Hall. 1985.

Hurwitz, Johanna. *Russell Rides Again.* Morrow. 1985.

Rosemarie Scotti Hughes, Ph.D. & Pamela C. Kloeppel, Ed.D.

This is My Friend

Objectives:

Drawing a picture to express feelings and experiences
To identify friends in daily life

Materials:

Drawing paper, crayons/markers.

Procedure:

1. Recall the characteristics of friends that we discussed in the previous session. Ask the children to close their eyes and think of a friend, either a child or an adult.
2. Next, ask them to draw a picture of this person.
3. When all have finished, ask volunteers to tell the group one thing this person does that makes them a friend.

Closure:

Summarize characteristics children have shared, and conclude that friends can be young or old, adult or child, of any color or size. What makes someone our friend is that he or she loves us and shows us that love. Ask the children for some ideas of how they can show love to others. Display pictures in classroom.

Sailing On:

Small children may still make up imaginary friends at this age, and this is no cause for alarm. However, pay attention to the child who makes up unbelievable friends (super rich or very powerful), and insists they are real, or to the one who cannot name a friend. These children may benefit from individual counseling.

Mooring Lines:

Boynton, Sandra. *Chloe and Maude.* Little, Brown. 1985.
Gibbs, Davis. *The Other Emily.* Houghton-Mifflin. 1984.

Rosemarie Scotti Hughes, Ph.D. & Pamela C. Kloeppel, Ed.D.

Peer Relationships
Kindergarten Session Three

Feeling Happy or Sad

Objectives:

Discussion of feelings when with others

Identification of these feelings

Materials:

Two pieces of construction paper, blue and yellow. The yellow sheet should have a happy face drawn on it, the blue a sad face.

Procedure:

1. "Sometimes when we are with people, we feel happy, and sometimes we feel sad. Close your eyes and remember a time when you were with a friend. Now open your eyes."

2. Ask for volunteers to share their thoughts. Then ask the volunteers to choose the face that shows how they felt during the experience. Ask why they felt either happy or sad.

Closure:

When all have responded, summarize the commonalities of the stories. You could ask the following:

"What is it that makes us happy when we are with others?"

"What is that makes us feel sad when we are with others?"

"What can we do so that others feel happy when they are around us?"

Sailing On:

Some classes may not at first identify sad experiences. If not, ask for volunteers to think of a sad time and share that. Also, you as the teacher could share a sad time you experienced as a child.

Listen carefully for children's stories of being sad. There may be some children who would benefit from further discussion with the school counselor. Children, too, can be depressed and need help.

If a child tells a story about abuse, do not question the child further in front of the class; jot down notes and follow legal procedures for reporting abuse. Further questioning may jeopardize any efforts by child protective services.

Children can draw pictures of their interactions and then discuss them.

You may want to use the blue and yellow circles on popsickle sticks from the earlier self-esteem lesson and have children vote on whether the story told was a happy or sad one. Then let the storyteller confirm or deny the vote.

Mooring Lines:

Weiss, Nicki. *Maude and Sally*. Glenwillow. 1983.

Winthrop, Elizabeth. *Katherine's Doll*. E.P. Dutton. 1983.

Winthrop, Elizabeth. *Lizzie and Harold*. Lothrop, Lee & Shepard. 1986.

Gordon, Shirley. *Crystal is My Friend*. Harper & Row. 1978.

To Share or Not to Share

Objectives:

Talking in a large group

Sharing as an aspect of friendship

Materials:

Drawing paper, crayons/markers.

Procedure:

1. Ask the children what sharing means. Have them recall times when they have shared with others, and when others have shared with them.

2. When they shared with others, was it always because they chose to share, or were they told to do so by an adult?

3. Did they always feel good about sharing? Were there times when they wanted to keep something for themselves but had to share anyway? Why did they not want to share?

4. Were there times when they felt good about sharing, when it made them feel happy to share? What was it that made them feel good? Was it the other person's happiness?

5. Have children draw a picture of themselves sharing something.

Closure:

Lead a discussion to wrap-up and summarize the children's comments. Sometimes it is easy to share and other times difficult. When we share and the other person is happy, then often we are happy. When we are selfish and do not share, we are thinking only of ourselves and not of others.

Sailing On:

Have the children, in another session, discuss the pictures they drew, and tell how they felt when sharing. How does sharing help another?

Display the pictures in the room as a reminder to share.

Mooring Lines:

Brown, Tricia. *Someone Special, Just Like You*. Holt. 1984.

McDonnell, Christine. *Don't Be Mad Ivy*. Dial. 1981.

Zolotow, Charlotte Shapiro. *The White Marble*. Thomas Y. Crowell. 1982.

Peer Relationships
Kindergarten Session Five

Share Week

Objectives:

Speaking in front of the class

Practice sharing

Materials:

"Award for Sharing" certificates (page 166), chart for recording sharing, with heading "Sharing S.A.I.L.S. us into friendship."

Procedure:

1. This is a week long activity that will require time to prepare children before you begin. Explain that this week will be a time to share. Each day, at the end of school, we will gather in a circle, and all will have a chance to tell how they shared something that day (or perhaps the day before, so you can include out-of-school time).

2. The sharing can be material, such as a treat from lunch, a toy with a friend, or lending a pencil or crayon to someone. The sharing can be of self—helping at home, giving time to a younger sibling, or being with a friend. Be sure that children understand all the ways they can share of themselves. You might want to make a list of suggestions and put them on a chart for display to remind the children. Children who do not yet read may benefit from having a chart with pictures of people sharing cut out from magazines.

3. As you have the circle each day, ask the children to tell their stories of sharing. Encourage and assist children to speak in complete sentences. Give each child who shares a certificate and mark the chart.

Closure:

Have a sharing party. Choose what is suitable for your class—you could collect canned goods for a food bank, make greeting cards for a nursing home or hospital, create a videotape of the children singing a special song to send to a nursing home, invite children from a special education class into your class for a story-time or songfest. Have refreshments as appropriate for your particular situation—snack time, or have parents help.

Mooring Lines:

Corey, Dorothy. *We All Share*. Albert Whitman. 1980.

Henkes, Kevin. *Chester's Way*. Puffin. 1988.

Lobel, Arnold. *Uncle Elephant*. Harper & Row. 1981.

Rosenberg, Maxine Berta. *My Friend Lease: The Story of a Handicapped Child*. Lothrop, Lee & Shepard. 1983.

Small's Favors. Modern Curriculum.

Award for
Sharing

Presented to

_____

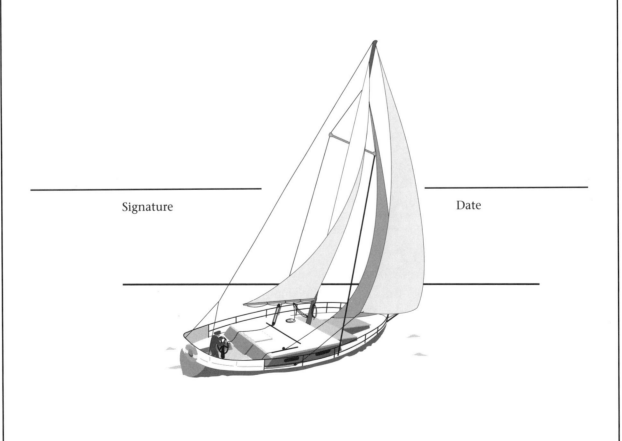

_____   _____
Signature   Date

_____

Rosemarie Scotti Hughes, Ph.D. & Pamela C. Kloeppel, Ed.D.

Peer Relationships
Kindergarten Session Six

A Friendly Graduation

Objectives:

Discussion of logical consequences

Identification of friendly characteristics in self

Materials:

"Official Friend Certificates" (page 168), appropriately filled in.

Procedure:

1. Explain that we have been working on being a friend for a long time in our class, and today is graduation day. (You may have to explain the meaning of the word, "graduation.") "You will each receive a graduation certificate, which will be special and unique for you. You will choose something special about yourself that I will write on your certificate."

2. Ask the children to orally complete the sentence, "A friend is someone who is...." As children give you descriptive words, write them on the board. If children give you a behavior rather than an adjective, help them formulate the behavior into a descriptive word.

3. Ask the children to look over the list, and choose one word which they think best describes them. Give help where needed, especially if children are not yet reading, and read the list to them so that they can pick the word.

4. Have certificates prepared for the children, and as you call each one, ask for the descriptive word he or she would like written on the certificate.

Closure:

After all have their certificates, ask how people respond to them when they act in ways described on their certificates, e.g., kind, helpful, polite, and so forth.

Sailing On:

If the children cannot ascribe a quality to themselves, ask their classmates to help.

You can use the certificates in many ways: They can be reduced in size on a copier so that the children can wear them as badges, they can be displayed in the room, or the children can make folders of construction paper so that they look like official diplomas.

You may want to have this lesson immediately after the sharing party described in the previous lesson.

Mooring Lines:

Hurwitz, Joanna. *Russell Rides Again*. William Morrow. 1985.

Krauss, Ruth. *I'll be You and You be Me*. HarperCollins Children's Books. 1988.

Marshall, James. *George and Martha Back in Town*. Houghton. 1984.

Ross, Pat. *Meet M & M*. Puffin. 1988.

Official Friend Certificate

_____

is a friend to others because

_____

_____ Teacher

_____ School

_____ Date

Official Friend Certificate

_____

is a friend to others because

_____

_____ Teacher

_____ School

_____ Date

Rosemarie Scotti Hughes, Ph.D. & Pamela C. Kloeppel, Ed.D.

Peer Relationships
First Grade Session One

We Are Good Friends

Objectives:

Development of language patterns through oral communication

Identifying characteristics a friendship

Materials:

"Butterfly Friendship Tags" (page 170).

Procedure:

1. Ask the children to think about a close friend and describe what is so special about that person. Ask how that person knows that he or she is your friend.

2. Discuss with the children how friends behave with one another. If they do not agree with one another, what do they do? When they are having a good time together, how do they act? What happens when two friends are together and a third person tries to join them?

3. Go around the room (or around the circle) and ask each child to tell one thing that he or she does to be a friend to others. As each child tells the action, give him a badge prepared with his or her name. Put badges on the children with pins or tape, and be sure to wear a badge yourself and tell how you are friendly.

Closure:

Remind the children that adults in the school are their friends, too: administrators, counselors, bus drivers, custodians, secretaries, cafeteria staff.

Emphasize that children can act friendly to all people in the school, students and staff alike.

Sailing On:

Introduce session with a recorded song about friends or a story about friends. You can repeat the song at the conclusion, or read the story as a follow up lesson.

Mooring Lines:

Christian, Mary Blount. *Penrod Again*. MacMillan. 1987.

Cohen, Miriam. *Jim's Dog Muffins*. Greenwillow. 1984.

Cohen, Miriam. *Liar Liar Pants on Fire*. Dell. 1987.

Scultz, Gwendolyn. *The Blue Valentine*. William Morrow. 1979.

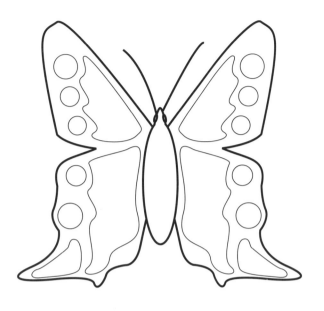

_____
is a good friend.

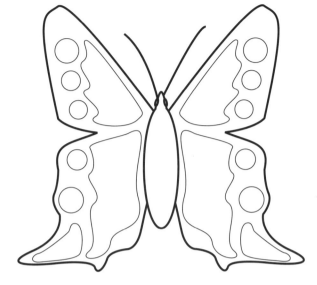

_____
is a good friend.

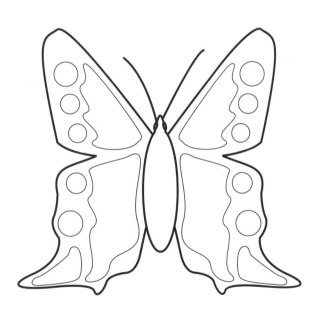

is a good friend.

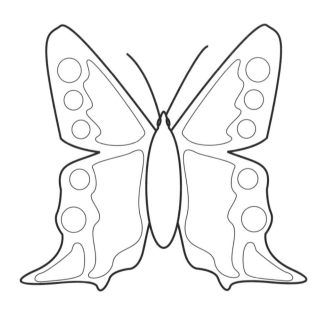

_____
is a good friend.

Rosemarie Scotti Hughes, Ph.D. & Pamela C. Kloeppel, Ed.D.

Peer Relationships
First Grade Session Two

Picture Gallery

Objectives:

Speaking in a large group

Recognition that people of all ages are our friends

Materials:

Drawing paper, crayons/markers.

Procedure:

1. Ask the children to close their eyes and think of a child who is their friend. When they think of the person they are to keep their eyes closed, but raise their hand. When all have raised their hands, tell children to open their eyes and discuss what these friends are like— who they are, and what makes them friends.

2. Repeat the procedure, but think of an adult who is a friend.

3. Distribute drawing paper and fold it in half. On each half draw the friends, on one side the adult, on the other side the child.

4. Each child can compile a "Friendship Book" beginning with the badge from the first session on the cover, and including each art activity. Some blank pages should be included for children to record friends' names, addresses, phone numbers (if children are allowed to do this), and other writing exercises about the pictures that they have drawn, as your time schedule permits.

Closure:

When drawings are complete, lead a discussion of how friends come in all shapes, sizes, both male and female, and all ages. Friendship has no limits.

Sailing On:

Be alert for children who cannot name a friend. These children may be shy or withdrawn and should be referred to the counselor.

Also be alert for children who discuss adult friends as someone with whom they have a secret. Adult molesters use "secrets" with children to indicate that they are special.

If you suspect any abuse, report it immediately to Child Protective Services and schedule the child for a counseling session.

Mooring Lines:

Marshall, James. *George and Martha*. Houghton-Mifflin. 1972.

Schick, Eleanor. *Peter and Mr. Brandon*. MacMillan. 1973.

McPhail, David. *Emma's Pet*. E.P. Dutton. 1985.

Thumbs Up, Thumbs Down

Objectives:

Recognition of synonyms and antonyms

Identification of friendly and unfriendly concepts

Materials:

Blackboard and chalk, or chartpaper and marker.

Procedure:

1. Write the word "friendly" on the board and ask the children to say the first word they think of when they see/hear this word.

2. After a number of children have given responses, repeat the procedure with the word, "unfriendly."

3. Explain that you are going to read a word to them and if the word means "friendly" then they are to give it a thumbs-up, if "unfriendly" then a thumbs-down. They are to have their eyes closed when you read the word, so that they are not influenced by each other.

4. Have two columns on board or paper, "Friendly and Unfriendly." When you read the word and children decide which it is, write it in the appropriate column. If the class is undecided, put it in a third column headed with a question mark, and return to it later. Discuss the "undecided" category, emphasizing why some feel one way and some another.

Word List:

loving	hateful	smiling	hugging
rough	kind	sharing	frowning
shaking hands	caring	mean	nasty
cheerful	giving	pleasant	helpful
warm	teasing	unpleasant	nice

Closure:

Review all words, asking children to use them in sentences orally.

Sailing On:

Add words from reading or spelling lists that are appropriate.

Have children use words in written sentences.

Mooring Lines:

Hanson, Joan. *Antonyms*. Learner. 1972.

Hanson, Joan. *Synonyms*. Learner. 1973.

Sarnoff, J. & Ruffins, R. *Words*. Charles Scribner's Sons. 1981.

Peer Relationships
First Grade Session Four

Friendly Hands

Objectives:

Using descriptive language

Friendly character strengths in self that facilitate friendship

Materials:

Drawing paper, crayons/markers, list of "friendly" words from previous session.

Procedure:

1. Review the "friendly" words from the previous session. Add other friendly words as children have them.

2. Have the children trace one hand on paper. In the center of the hand, they are to write their name. Then, on the thumb and each finger, they are to write one quality that makes them a good friend (five words in all).

Closure:

Gather the children into a circle with their hand tracings; have all read their "hands" individually, saying, "I am a good friend because I ...." Display the hands around room.

Mooring Lines:

Lobel, Arnold. *Frog and Toad All Year*. Harper & Row. 1976.

Lobel, Arnold. *Frog and Toad Together*. Harper & Row. 1972.

Pryor, B. *Amanda and April*. William Morrow. 1986.

Fun With My Friends

Objectives:

Oral expression of realistic or imaginative stories

The value of friends

Materials:

Drawing paper, crayons/markers.

Procedure:

1. Remind the children of past discussions and activities about friends. Refer to the friendly hands drawings. Ask the children to think of an activity that they would like to do with their friends. Anything is acceptable, such as a trip to Mars, a party at the bottom of the sea or the top of a volcano. Activities can be real or imaginary.

2. After volunteers relate their stories, ask why it would be important to have friends along on these trips. Would they be as much fun without friends? How do friends make occasions special?

3. Do our friends make everyday activities special, e.g., watching TV, listening to music, or playing games?

4. Have children draw pictures of things that they do or would like to do with their friends.

Closure:

Have the children discuss how their lives are happier/richer because of their friends. What do they do to keep these friendships? (e.g., Play together, help each other, share, listen to problems?)

Summarize by saying, "To have friends, you have to be a friend; you often have to take the first step to be a friend as well as help a friend when times are difficult. Then when you need help, your friend will do the same for you."

Mooring Lines:

Watson, Wendy. *Wendy Watson's Mother Goose*. Lothrop, Lee & Shepard. 1989.

Wells, Rosemary. *Timothy Goes to School*. Dial. 1981.

Spinelli, E. *Somebody Loves You Mr. Hatch*. Bradbury. 1991.

Wells, Rosemary. *Benjamin and Tulip*. Dial. 1973.

Rosemarie Scotti Hughes, Ph.D. & Pamela C. Kloeppel, Ed.D.

Peer Relationships
First Grade Session Six

Sail Into Friendship

Objectives:

Recognition of words that facilitate friendship

Choosing behaviors that will help children be friends to others

Materials:

Large picture of sailboat (page 176), pencils, crayons/markers.

Procedure:

1. Explain that this is the last session we will have about friendship, and we will work on the last page of our friendship books. (See page 171.) Distribute the picture of a sailboat.

2. Ask the children to think of a name for their boat that would describe it as a special boat of friendship. Allow ample time for children to share, and have them write the name of their boat on the bow.

3. Next, remind them that a sailboat can only move when the wind is blowing, and that the line from the top of the sail represents a friendly wind. Ask the children what they can do at school and at home that will make their friendship boat sail smoothly. List these on the board or on chartpaper as the children give them to you.

4. Next, ask the children to choose one behavior that they agree to do in the coming week to make their friendship boat sail, and write this word on the line to make sure the wirds are friendly.

Closure:

Ask the children to share their chosen "wind" and what they hope will happen when they act out this positive behavior.

Sailing On:

Children can write follow up sentences daily in their friendship books about a positive behavior they have shown the day before, or that day in school.

A large model sailboat, or poster, can be placed in the room with pictures of children and a slogan as a reminder to be friendly with one another, such as "We're sailing into friendship."

Mooring Lines:

Berger, Terry. *Friends*. Simon & Schuster. 1981.

Modell, Frank. *One Zillion Valentines*. Greenwillow. 1981.

Rogers, Fred. *Making Friends*. Putnam's Sons. 1987.

Rosemarie Scotti Hughes, Ph.D. & Pamela C. Kloeppel, Ed.D.

Peer Relationships
Second Grade Session One

Be a Friend Today

Objectives:

Oral expression of cause and effect

Actions that show friendship

Materials:

"Today Is Be A Friend Day" badges (page 178), blackboard and chalk, or chartpaper and markers.

Procedure:

1. Explain that today is "Be a Friend" day, and that we will all wear special badges and do special things today to show others that we are friendly.

2. Ask the children to discuss what they can do in school to show others that they are friendly. Explore possibilities in the classroom, the halls, playground, buses, cafeteria, and walking to and from home.

3. Ask each child to state a sentence about what he or she can do today to show friendship, identifying what will happen afterwards. You can use examples: "When I walk quietly down the hall, I will not disturb others' lessons," or "When I wait for my turn on the playground, we will have a better game."

4. Write sentences down as children state them. As a role model, state your own activity today and wear your badge also.

Closure:

Give the children badges to wear. Save closure until the end of the day when you review activities and find out what happened when the children performed friendly acts.

Sailing On:

This may be a time to review what it is like being new in a school, and ask if there is a way we can help new students.

This activity can be done in small groups, if you have a large class, with the groups deciding on one action for all members to do. These actions could be designed to help the class run more smoothly or deal with a special problem.

Mooring Lines:

Fair, Sylvia. *The Bedspread*. Morrow Jr. 1982.

Hughes, Shirley. *Dogger*. Lothrop, Lee & Shepard. 1988.

Levy, Elizabeth. *Nice Little Girls*. Delacourte. 1978.

Peet, Bill. *Cowardly Clyde*. Houghton-Mifflin. 1984.

Peet, Bill. *Encore for Eleanor*. Houghton-Mifflin. 1985.

Peet, Bill. *Jennifer and Josephine*. Houghton-Mifflin. 1980.

TODAY IS BE A FRIEND DAY

TODAY IS BE A FRIEND DAY

TODAY IS BE A FRIEND DAY

TODAY IS BE A FRIEND DAY

Rosemarie Scotti Hughes, Ph.D. & Pamela C. Kloeppel, Ed.D.

**Peer Relationships
Second Grade Session Two**

Red and Blue Balloons

Objectives:

Word recognition

Attitude, actions, and qualities that do or do not promote harmony among people

Materials:

Balloon handout (page 180), crayons/markers.

Procedure:

1. Remind the children that the last time you discussed friendship you talked about friendly acts and everyone tried to do friendly things. However, sometimes we and other people do not act in a friendly way.

2. "Today we are going to look at balloons that have words on them, both friendly and unfriendly words. If a balloon has a word that makes you think of a friendly person, color it blue; if unfriendly, color it red."

3. Review the words with the class one at a time.

4. As words are being colored, have volunteers use a word in a sentence.

Closure:

Discuss which words the children liked better—which qualities would they rather have people show towards them, and which would they like to show to others.

Sailing On:

Make up a sheet of balloons with appropriate words from reading or spelling lists.

As children give their sentences, write them on board or chartpaper and have children copy them later.

Make up a class story using some of the words.

Ask the children to write a short poem with one of the words.

Mooring Lines:

Steig, William. *Amos and Boris.* Farrar, Straus & Giroux. 1971.

McLerran, Alice. *Roxaboxen.*

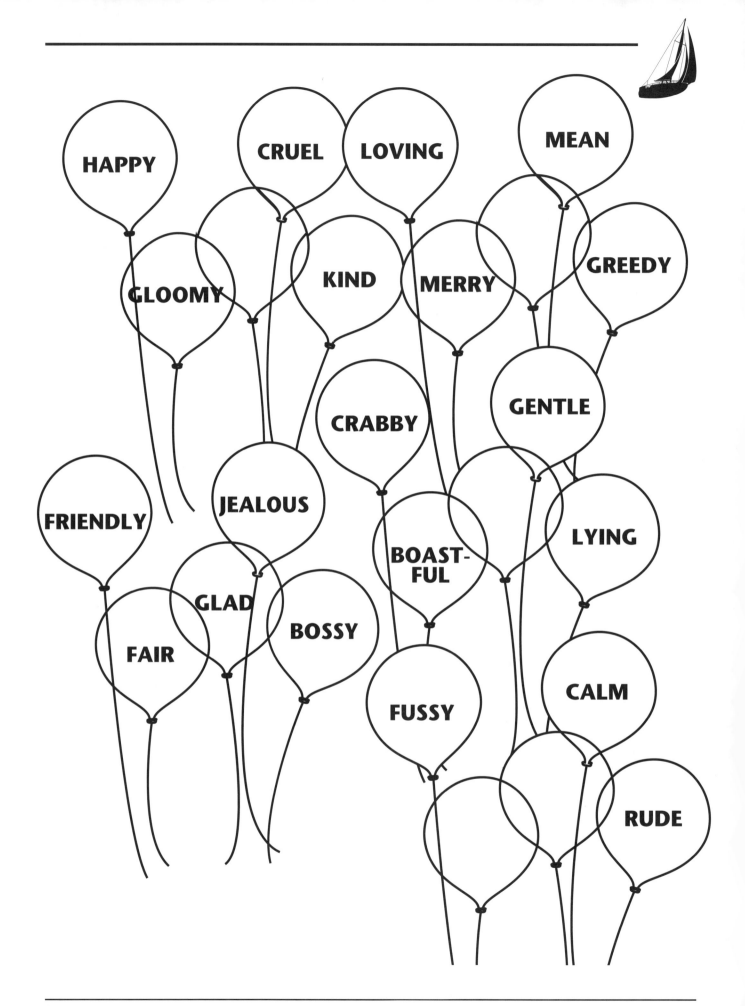

Rosemarie Scotti Hughes, Ph.D. & Pamela C. Kloeppel, Ed.D.

Peer Relationships
Second Grade Session Three

Who Needs Manners?

Objectives:

Creating an ending for a story
Value of good manners

Materials:

Stories on the following page

Procedure:

1. Ask a child to read the definition of "manners" from the dictionary. Then ask some children to use the word "manners" in a sentence, using the definition that refers to customs or ways of doing things.

2. Ask for times when they have good manners.

3. Ask for times when adults remind them to have good manners, when they are told to "mind your manners."

4. Lead a brief discussion on why manners are important:
   — to know what to do in new situations
   — to help people feel comfortable
   — to be gracious and kind to others.

5. Explain that you are going to read some short stories (or if appropriate, to have children read them) that have no endings; the class is to provide the endings. Each story can have more than one ending.

6. Read each story, and list all possible endings that the children offer on the board.

Closure:

Review each story, and have the class choose the ending that shows the best manners.

Sailing On:

After all stories are read, role play the stories with their different endings.

You may wish to read a story, generate several endings, and role play each story/ending, focusing on one story each day.

This activity can be done with a whole class or with a small group, such as a reading group. There may be stories in the reader that have some alternative endings that could be acted out.

Mooring Lines:

Behrens, June. *Manners Book.* Golden Gate Children's. 1980.

Ephron, Delia. *Do I Have to Say Hello? Aunt Delia's Manners Quiz for Kids and Their Grown-ups.* Viking. 1989.

Krensky, Stephen. *Perfect Pigs: An Introduction to Manners.*

Leaf, Munro. *Manners Can Be Fun.* HarperCollins Children's. 1985.

Parish, Peggy. *Mind Your Manners.* Greenwillow. 1978.

Session Three Stories

1. Janice and Marsha are walking towards the door at school. Janice is carrying a large bag which contains her costume for the class play. She is also carrying some books and a lunchbox. Marsha is carrying one book. When they come to the closed door....

2. Roberto and Andrew are in line for lunch. Andrew suddenly remembers that he left his lunch ticket in his desk and asks permission to go back and get it. When he comes back to the lunchroom, Andrew asks Roberto if he may have his place back in line, and....

3. Harry and Joshua are friends. Their class is playing softball today. Harry is not a very good ballplayer, but Joshua is. When it is Harry's turn to bat, he swings three times in a row and is out. Some of the children laugh at him, but Joshua....

4. Denise is at a party with her friend, Natalie. There are trays of cookies from which the children may choose what they would like. Denise has a big chocolate chip cookie on her plate already, and Natalie decides that she would like one also. Just then, someone reaches ahead of Natalie and takes the last big chocolate chip cookie. Denise....

5. Sally and Tommy are in the grocery store when a lady in the aisle with them drops several cans of corn. Sally and Tommy....

Rosemarie Scotti Hughes, Ph.D. & Pamela C. Kloeppel, Ed.D.

Peer Relationships
Second Grade Session Four
Cooperation is the Name of the Game

Objectives:

Discovering cause and effect in personal communication

Benefits of cooperative behavior

Materials:

Large sheets of drawing paper (chartpaper size), and regular sized sheets of drawing paper, crayons/markers/paint.

"Winner" badges (page 184).

Procedure:

1. Have a volunteer read the dictionary definition of "cooperate." Ask the children for examples of cooperation that they see at home and/ or school. Have a brief discussion on how it feels to cooperate with others, or have others cooperate with you.

2. Divide the children into groups of four. For half of the groups, distribute regular-sized paper. Give large sheets of drawing paper to the other half. Instruct the groups with the regular-sized paper that each child is to draw one picture of whatever they choose. Instruct the groups with large paper for each group to work together to create one picture. Give a time limit, and offer a prize for the best picture.

3. When the time is up, discuss the activity and ask which group had the most enjoyable time—those who worked together or those who worked alone. Why?

Closure:

Explain that all are winners, and give out badges to all. Discuss the pictures—which does the class like better, the group picture or the individual picture. Ask what they learned about cooperating towards a goal, in this case, a prize.

Sailing On:

Repeat the activity, switching groups.

Mooring Lines:

Brandenberg, Franz. *Nice New Neighbors*. Greenwillow. 1977.

Gackenbach, Dick. *Claude and Pepper*. Houghton-Mifflin. 1979.

_____
is a
Winner

_____
is a
Winner

_____
is a
Winner

_____
is a
Winner

Rosemarie Scotti Hughes, Ph.D. & Pamela C. Kloeppel, Ed.D.

Peer Relationships
Second Grade Session Five
That's What Friends are For!

Objectives:

Oral storytelling

Value of shared activities among friends

Materials:

Drawing paper, crayons and/or markers, pencils and lined paper, blackboard and chalk, or chartpaper and markers.

Procedure:

1. Discuss why it is more fun to do some activities with friends than to do them alone. Ask the children to give examples of activities they enjoy doing with their friends.

2. Explain that today the class will write a story together about friends. Let the class choose the names of three of four make believe friends. Brainstorm ideas for the setting and locale. Next, proceed to write the story on the board.

3. Divide the class into three groups. The first group will draw a picture about something that happened in the beginning of the story, the second group about something that happened in the middle of the story, and the third group about something that happened at the end.

4. When children have completed drawing, choose one child from each group to come to the front to display and discuss their drawing sequentially.

Closure:

Point out the different interpretations that each group made in their drawing; the characters and settings all looked different, even though it was the same story. Friends are of all types, and what is important is how we feel when we are together, not what we/they look like.

Sailing On:

You can assign children in groups of three to work cooperatively on writing and then drawing a sequential story in a subsequent lesson.

You may want to work on character development more intensely, having the story characters developed in detail before the children begin writing.

Mooring Lines:

Barkin, Carol & James, Elizabeth. *Are We Still Best Friends*. Raintree. 1975.

Cohen, Miriam. *Best Friends*. MacMillan. 1971

Hallinan, P.K. *That's What a Friend Is*. Children's.

When Friends Disagree

Objectives:

Sentence writing

Finding alternatives to fighting

Materials:

Lined paper and pencils, blackboard and chalk, or chartpaper and markers.

Procedure:

1. Ask the children what they do when they disagree with their friends—how do they solve their differences? Allow time for a variety of answers—leave, talk it out, hit the other person, argue, get another friend involved to settle it.

2. When the discussion is ended, explain that today we are going to look at ways to solve differences with our friends so that we remain friends. Put two columns on the board, "Helping" and "Hurting."

3. Ask the children to brainstorm ways to solve differences and choose which column is appropriate.

4. Have the children choose one helpful way of solving a difference and one hurtful way; then write a sentence about what would happen in each situation.

5. Have the volunteers read their sentences aloud.

Closure:

Lead the class in a discussion of which method of solving problems leads to peaceful solutions. Some may believe fighting or arguing as solving the problem, but point out the friendship is lost and the problems are never solved.

Mooring Lines:

Giff, Patricia Reilly. *Happy Birthday, Ronald Morgan*. Viking. 1986.

Kellogg, Steven. *Best Friends*. Dial. 1986.

Levine, Abby & Levine, Sarah. *Sometimes I Wish I Were Mindy*. Albert Whitman. 1986.

Sharmat, Marjorie. *Atilla the Angry*. Holiday House. 1985.

Sharmat, Marjorie. *Bartholomew the Bossy*. MacMillan. 1984.

Winthrop, Elizabeth. *Katherine's Doll*. Puffin. 1991.

Peer Relationships
Third Grade Session One

Friendly Certificates

Objectives:

Improve speaking and writing skills

Identify friendship qualities

Materials:

Index cards, elementary dictionary, "Sail into Friendship Certificates" (page 188), with children's names written in the proper space.

Procedure:

1. Explain to the children that today we are going to say only good things about ourselves and about each other. We are going to learn about our good qualities.

2. Have a student read the definition of a "quality" from the elementary dictionary.

3. Distribute index cards; have children write their names and one good quality about themselves on the card.

4. Next, have the children exchange cards with someone. Ask them to turn the cards over and write one good thing about the person whose name is on the card. Return cards to original owners.

5. Ask the children to stand and read their two good qualities to the class. "I am (name), and I am _____ and _____."

Closure:

Explain that the qualities we just identified are the same qualities that help us get along with others. Tell the students that for the next five weeks they will have special activities about getting along with others. Today they will each receive a friendship certificate. Distribute the certificates (fill in "teacher" or "counselor," "school," and "date" before running copies) to the students and have them complete using the quality on the index card they like best. Display the certificates in the room.

"All of us have qualities that people like. We learned about these qualities today. We use these qualities both at home and school. The more friendship qualities we use, the more people will like us and the better we will get along with others."

Sailing On:

The students can take their certificates home. They are to ask an adult in their home when they exhibited this characteristic; they are to describe this incident on the back of their certificate and share it with the class the next day. After sharing their certificate incidents, display their certificates in the room.

Mooring Lines:

Coutant, Helen. *The Gift.* Alfred A. Knopf. 1983.

Gibbs, Davis. *The Other Emily.* Houghton-Mifflin. 1984.

Giff, Patricia Reilly. *Fish Face.* Dell. 1984.

Hautzig, Deborah. *Why Are You So Mean to Me?* Random House. 1986.

Hopkins, Lee. *Best Friends.* Harper. 1986.

Winthrop, Elizabeth. *Lizzie & Harold.* Lothrop, Lee & Shepard. 1986.

Sail Into Friendship Certificate

_____

is a friend who _____

_____

_____ Mother

_____ Teacher

_____ School

_____ Date

Kind and loving acts are the sails which carry us into friendship.

Sail Into Friendship Certificate

_____

is a friend who _____

_____

_____ Mother

_____ Teacher

_____ School

_____ Date

Kind and loving acts are the sails which carry us into friendship.

Rosemarie Scotti Hughes, Ph.D. & Pamela C. Kloeppel, Ed.D.

Peer Relationships
Third Grade Session Two

Friendly Town

Objectives:

Complete a creative writing assignment

Understand that friendly behavior can improve classroom environment

Materials:

Construction paper, markers, blackboard and chalk, or chart paper.

Procedure:

1. Ask the children the name of the city where they live; write it on the board. Then ask the names of the streets where the students live. Write these on the board.

2. Ask if they know who runs the city—is there a mayor? A city council? Who takes care of the people in the city—police officers? fire fighters? sanitation workers? superintendent of schools? and so forth. (Be prepared with names of officials—cities often have free brochures with this information.)

3. Explain that today our classroom is going to become a city with streets and people to help run the town. Tell the children that the classroom will, for the next five weeks, be named "Friendly Town."

4. Ask the students what this name means. From the discussion, choose street names that reflect friendly qualities for the rows of desks. Have children make "street signs" for each row of tables or groupings, to accommodate the class organization. Put up street signs and leave them in place for next five weeks.

5. Discuss how people work together in a "Friendly Town." How do they act toward each other? What do people do to keep their streets clean? What do they do to feel proud about their town?

Closure:

"There are differences in our imagined friendly town and our real neighborhoods. We may be able to make small changes in our neighborhood by doing something good for the neighborhood. But in our class we can make a big difference; we can make our class really become 'Friendly Town' by acting the way we said friendly town people would act." Conclude by having the children shake hands with all of the people on their street, saying, "Hi, Neighbor, I am glad I live in a 'Friendly Town!' I'm glad you are my neighbor."

Sailing On:

Assign creative writing in which the students explain one or more similarity/difference in "Friendly Town" and in their own neighborhoods. They are also to tell which town/neighborhood they like best and why.

This session could be the introduction to a unit on local or state government.

Mooring Lines:

Baylor, Bryd. *The Best Town in the World.* Macmillan. 1983.

Carlson, Nancy Lee. *Loudmouth George & the Sixth Grade*

Jordan, June. *Kimako's Story.* Houghton-Mifflin. 1981.

Knox-Wagner, Elaine. *An Apartment's No Place for a Kid.* Whitman. 1985.

Schotter, Roni. *Efan the Great.* Lothrop, Lee & Shepard.

Rosemarie Scotti Hughes, Ph.D. & Pamela C. Kloeppel, Ed.D.

Peer Relationships
Third Grade Session Three

This is Our Town

Objectives:

Write a paragraph(s)

To understand that friendly behavior can improve classroom and neighborhood environments

Materials:

Drawing paper, crayons and/or markers, pencils and writing paper.

Procedure:

1. Group the students by streets from last week's session.

2. Remind students about the "Friendly Town" they created in the classroom during the last session. Pointing to the street signs they created, ask the students to think of some good things people in a neighborhood can do together—things that will help the neighborhood or improve relationships between neighbors, e.g., have a picnic or a clean-up day, recycle newspapers, plant a garden, take food to a sick person, and so forth.

   Ask the groups to decide on a friendly activity for their classroom. Remind the students about a model of decision making if they have experienced the decision making lessons (*D.E.C.I.D.E./S.A.I.L./D.O.G.*, page 193).

4. When the task is completed, ask each group to report on their chosen activity.

5. Make plans to do these activities in class during the school year; one activity a month may be a good schedule.

Closure:

We know we can make a difference when we do friendly things—here at school, at home, and in our neighborhood. All we have to do is try. When we do friendly things we help other people. When we do friendly things, other people like us and we like ourselves.

Sailing On:

Assign each student a paragraph about a friendly act he or she can undertake in his or her neighborhood. This can be a one time activity or an on-going one. Have him or her explain the steps to be taken. Explain that our parents or the adults we live with might have lots of good ideas about completing this project. Encourage communication at home. Request parental written permission on the student's paragraph, if the activity is to carried out.

If they are afraid to do anything friendly in their neighborhood because of the violence, have them do something friendly within their home.

Mooring Lines:

Bulla, Clyde R. *Shoeshine Girl.* Thomas Y. Crowell. 1975.

Cleary, Beverly. *Henry & the Paper Route.* William Morrow. 1957.

DeRegniers, Beatrice. *The Way I Feel. . .Sometimes.* Ticknor & Fields. 1988.

Martin, Charles. *Summer Business.* Greenwillow. 1984.

Showas, Paul. *Where Does the Garbage Go?* Harper & Row. 1974.

Friendly Town Resolutions

Objectives:

Creative writing about a friendship resolution

Implement friendship resolutions in class

Materials:

Elementary dictionary, blackboard and chalk, chartpaper and marker, paper and pencil

Procedure:

1. Write the word "resolutions" on the board, and ask the children if anyone knows the meaning of the word. Ask if they have ever heard of New Year's resolutions. Explain that a resolution is not exactly a law, but a statement that someone intends to do something.

2. Have a volunteer read the dictionary definition of "resolution".

3. Tell the children, "There are so many people in our "Friendly Town" with good friendship qualities that we can now agree on "Friendly Town Resolutions." These resolutions will help us be friendly to others.

4. There are a few things to remember—resolutions are not to include "do not;" rather, they are to be things to DO. Each resolution should be about one thing. For example, "Greet others with a smile," would be a Friendly Town Resolution. Generate a resolution list of positive behaviors with the children. Put these on the board or on a large sheet of paper to post in the room.

5. Have the class vote on one or two resolutions to undertake, and discuss the steps which are needed to accomplish this task.

Closure:

Good deeds and good activities bring people together; we learn through them to trust and depend on each other. When trust and dependency develops in a group, the group becomes a community. Our class is becoming a community. In this community we can trust and depend on each other.

Sailing On:

Assign as homework creative writing about a positive behavior identified but not selected. How could such behavior be implemented in the classroom?

After reading the papers contact any student who has identified good strategies you may want to incorporate in the class. Have a "town meeting" for these students to read their papers and be voted on as potential additional resolutions.

Mooring Lines:

Anglund, Joan. *A Friend is Someone Who Likes You*. Harcourt. 1958.

DePaola, Tomie. *Oliver Button is a Sissy*. Harbrace. 1990.

Greenfield, Eloise. *Honey, I Love and Other Love Poems*. Harper & Row. 1978.

Hughes, Sally. *Moving Molly*. Lothrop, Lee & Shepard. 1988.

Silverstein, Shel. *The Giving Tree*. Harper & Row.

Peer Relationships
Third Grade Session Five

Bumper Stickers

Objectives:

Writing a motto/slogan about being friendly

Understanding the consequences of being friendly

Materials:

Car bumper stickers, resolutions from previous sessions, drawing paper, pencils, markers and/or crayons, glitters, and other appropriate art materials.

Procedure:

1. Show the children a few examples of car bumper stickers; use a school bumper sticker, if available. Explain that a bumper sticker doesn't have a lot of room, so the designer must give an important message in a few words. For example, "Smile—and get one back!" Such messages are called mottos or slogans.

2. Discuss the resolutions that were developed in the previous session and any changes which have come about in "Friendly Town" because of resolutions or other friendly behavior. For example, if you greet people with a smile, what do they usually do? Smile back!

3. Ask each child to create a bumper sticker with a friendly behavior and its consequences.

4. Ask each student to explain his or her bumper sticker message. Display bumper stickers in the room.

Closure:

Today we made bumper stickers about the consequences of being friendly. Are these consequences good for us? How? Are these consequences good for others? How? By being friendly we help ourselves and others. We make our world and that of the people around us, better.

Sailing On:

Consider a ballot-type election to choose the three best bumper stickers.

Use this session as an introduction to a unit on advertising through various media.

Mooring Lines:

Brown, Marc. *The True Francine*. Little, Brown. 1981.

Hurwitz, Johanna. *Yellow Blue Jay*. Morrow. 1986.

Porte, Ann Barbara. *Harry's Visit*. Greenwillow. 1983.

Smith, Doris Buchanan. *Last Was Lloyd*. Viking. 1981.

Secret Pal

Objective:

Creative writing about changed behavior

Understand that friendly acts are the beginning of friendship

Materials:

Paper, pencils, name and birth date of each child written on one index card and placed in a show box, chalk and chalkboard.

Procedure:

1. Ask the children how the classroom has changed since we have become "Friendly Town." Write these changes on the board.

2. Have the class vote on the three changes they like the best; see if the class will agree to continue these changed behaviors for the rest of the year.

3. Have the students write a paragraph, poem, song, rap, and so forth about one change, either in their own behavior or in someone else's, which has been important to them. This can be homework.

4. Ask for volunteers to share their writings.

5. Collect for review.

6. Explain that each child will draw a name of a "secret pal." "A secret pal is a person who looks out for someone else without this person knowing who he or she is. One person helps another without revealing his or her identity. At certain times, secret pals do something special for their assigned friend. We are going to be extra friendly to our "secret pal" all year. How can we do this?" Generate ideas (holding the door open, helping to carry things, making a card for his or her birthday, including in a game, etc.)

7. "On the last day of school, during our class party, we will identify all secret pals."

Closure:

We have learned about being friends for the last six weeks. We have turned our classroom into "Friendly Town." Our friendly acts help other people feel more comfortable and cared for. They in turn care more for us and treat us with kindness and respect. Friendly acts results in friendship, trust and interdependence among people. Friendly acts begin the circle of friendship:

Rosemarie Scotti Hughes, Ph.D. & Pamela C. Kloeppel, Ed.D.

Friendship Circle

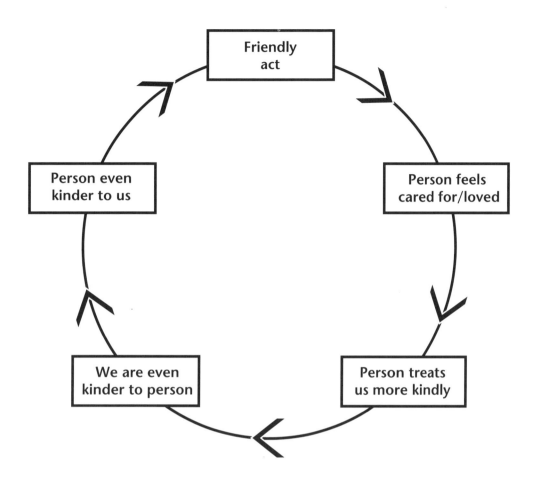

Sailing On:

Other options for secret pals are:

> a gift (bought or made from school supplies), at Hanukkah/ Christmas
>
> a valentine on Valentine's Day
>
> at Easter, a decorated egg
>
> on a Secret Pal's birthday, a homemade card or small gift
>
> a picture of the friend with a nice saying

Make a calendar to remind students in advance of birthday remembrances.

You may also want to have a secret pal center or general store available in the classroom where students can bring in crafts and materials to create gifts; this center will also help those without resources at home.

Mooring Lines:

DeClements, Barthe. *Nothing's Fair in Fifth Grade.* Viking. 1981.
Lise, Janet Taylor. *Afternoon of the Elves.* Orchard. 1989.
Sharmat, Marjorie Weinman. *Who's Afraid of Ernestine?* Coward-McCann. 1986.

Official Friends

Objectives:

Improve reading and writing skills

Identify the qualities of a friend

Materials:

Dictionary, "Official Friend Certificates" (page 197).

Procedure:

1. Ask the children to give definitions for the word, "friend."
2. After the children's definition ask for a volunteer to read the definition of "friend" from the dictionary.
3. Now ask for words that have the same meaning as friend (buddy, pal, classmate). Allow children to use street slang if they wish.
4. Ask the students to give examples of these words in their own lives.
5. Discuss the difference between being a friend and being friendly. "Are they friends with everyone, many people, or few people? Are they friendly with a lot of people or a few people? Is there a difference between being a friend and being friendly?" After the students understand the difference, ask "Is easy or hard to be a friend?"
6. Explain, "Today you are going to write a description of your best friend—not what he or she looks like, but the inside qualities that cause you to like this person." The description can take any creative writing form.
7. When finished, ask each child to read his or her writing aloud.

Closure:

Look for themes in the students' reports and point them out, i.e., our class thinks being kind and sharing is important in a friend. We like friends who listen. End by saying, "We have identified some common characteristics our class likes in friends. You can see that it isn't just one thing that makes a friend. It is many different things. Many acts of kindness, many times to listen, many instances of sharing. How do you rate as a friend?"

As a culmination, distribute the "Official Friend" Certificates" which you have previously completed. Explain to children that in the next five weeks they will be participating in activities about friendship.

Sailing On:

Have the students create a word find around the theme of friendship. This can be done individually or in small groups.

Mooring Lines:

Giff, Patricia Reilly. *Fish Face.* Dell. 1984.

Lobel, Arnold. *Frog and Toad* (Series). Harper Collins Children's. 1972.

Marshall, James. *George & Martha* (Series). Houghton-Mifflin. 1972.

Martin, Anne Mathews. *Stage Fright.* Holiday House. 1984.

Sherra, Mary Francis Craig. *Chester.* Putnam. 1980.

Rosemarie Scotti Hughes, Ph.D. & Pamela C. Kloeppel, Ed.D.

Official Friend Certificate

_____
School Name

_____
Student's Name

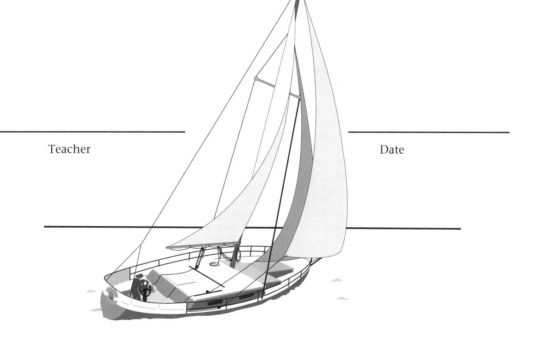

_____   _____
Teacher   Date

_____

Kind and loving acts are the sails which carry us into friendship.

Problems, Problems

Objectives:

Improve oral and writing skills

Develop strategies to handle peer pressure

Materials:

Dictionary, "Decision Questions" (page 199) and "Problem Situations" (page 200).

Procedure:

1. Group the children in threes.

2. Ask the children if they have ever been in a situation where a friend wanted them to do something they didn't think they should do? Ask the children to share what they did in these circumstances and what happened afterward. Was it harder to say "NO" than to say "YES"?

3. Explain that this is called "peer pressure" by adults; have a student read the dictionary definition of "peer" and then make sure they understand "peer pressure".

4. Tell the group they will discuss some problem situations, and find ways to say "No" to friends. They will use the "Decision Questions" handout to decide whether to say "yes" or "no" to the problem situation.

5. Assign one problem to each group. Tell the groups they are to make a report to the class by answering each question on the "Decision Questions" handout. Give them at least fifteen minutes to discuss the problem and answer questions in their group.

6. After each group report, ask for comments from the other students on what they would do.

Closure:

"We all have peer pressure to do things that are not the best for us. Even as adults we still have pressure to do things that are not in our best interest. But peer pressure is harder to resist when you are a teen because teenagers want to be liked so much by others. This need to be liked makes you susceptible to peer pressure. You may believe that being liked is more important than doing what is right. Always ask yourself, 'Is it right for me? Will it help me be better and accomplish my goals?'"

Sailing On:

Assign a class or homework writing sample on one peer pressure problem identified by a student. How would the student solve it, using the "Decision Questions?" After reviewing for writing and skills in logic, place the paper in student's portfolio. Show the video "Vultures" as the culminating class activity and assign writing for homework.

Discuss peer pressure through marketing, e.g., cigarette ads with beautiful people, diet drinks to be slim, gum so people will like to be with you. Have students bring examples to class and discuss.

Mooring Lines:

Gould, Marilyn. *Golden Daffodils.* Addison-Wesley. 1982.

Hogan, Paula Z. *I Hate Boys, I Hate Girls.* Raintree. 1980.

Hurwitz, Johanna. *The Hot and Cold Summer.* Morrow. 1984.

Rosemarie Scotti Hughes, Ph.D. & Pamela C. Kloeppel, Ed.D.

Decision Questions

1. What is the problem?

_____

_____

_____

2. What will happen if you say yes?

_____

_____

_____

3. What will happen if you say no?

_____

_____

_____

4. What makes it hard for the person to say "No"?

_____

_____

_____

5. What would you do in the situation?

_____

_____

_____

Problem Situations

A. You have permission from your parents to attend a movie at the mall. When you get there, all of your friends want to go to another movie that your parents have forbidden you to see.

B. You are in a convenience store with a friend for a soft drink. Outside, you see a teenager give an adult money to buy him beer. Your friend says that this is a good idea and wants to get someone to buy beer also.

C. You have become friends with someone at school who doesn't live in your neighborhood. Your old friends do not like this person and tell you that they will no longer be your friend if you continue your new friendship.

D. You have a lot of homework tonight. A very popular classmate calls you to come over to watch a movie. Your mother says you can go, when you have finished your homework. You want to go watch the movie, because the person who called you has never asked you to do anything before. You think that you have time after the movie to finish the homework.

E. Two of your best friends have decided to cut school the last Friday of May. It is a beautiful day and they ask you to go with them to the beach.

F. One of the school leaders lives next door to you but you two have never been close friends. At school, during a test, he asks to look at the answers on your paper.

G. A fifth grade friend asks you to go to a concert with him in his father's car. Then you find out he plans to drive the car himself since his parents will be out of town.

Rosemarie Scotti Hughes, Ph.D. & Pamela C. Kloeppel, Ed.D.

Peer Relationships
Fourth Grade Session Three

Lights, Camera, Action

Objectives:

Dramatize peer pressure problems and appropriate responses

Develop strategies to handle peer pressure

Materials:

Each situation from the preceding session, cut out and put on index cards. If available, some suitable props.

Procedure:

1. Divide class into equally-numbered groups.

2. Recall last session's discussion about how to say "No" to friends in peer pressure situations. Explain that today we are going to act out these situations so we can practice telling people "No" when we need to do so.

3. Distribute index cards, so that one problem situation is given to each group. Give groups ten minutes to plan what they will do; they will have to choose actors, perhaps a narrator and plan the role play.

4. After all the role plays, lead the class in a discussion of similarity and differences of each role play approach. End each role play by discussing the question, "How can you be hurt when you say "yes" (or helped when you say "no") in this situation?

Closure:

"Peer pressure is not easy to handle, but there are ways to handle it, just as we have seen today. Peer pressure is easier to handle by always asking and answering, 'How will I be hurt or helped if I say yes; will I be hurt or helped if I say no.' Also ask yourself if your parents or grandparents would approve. Always go with the response that will hurt you the least in the long run, the response that will help you be successful in the future.'

Sailing On:

You might want to role-play additional situations. You can use peer pressure situations the children related in the last session or others which you have encountered in class.

Mooring Lines:

Conford, Ellen. *Anything for a Friend*. Little, Brown. 1979.
Honeycutt, Natalie. *Invisible Lisa*. Bradbury. 1985.

Gossip

Objectives:

Improve reading and writing skills

Understand that gossip and rumor can hurt others as well as self

Materials:

Dictionary.

Procedure:

1. Have the group sit in a circle.

2. Explain that today we are going to play the game, "Gossip." Ask for a volunteer to read, in a whisper, the message below, in the ear of the next person; the last person to receive the message will say it out aloud. Then the first person repeats what he originally said.

> **MESSAGE: VIRGINIA IS ON THE EAST COAST OF THE UNITED STATES, ON THE ATLANTIC OCEAN. THE CAPITAL IS RICHMOND. THE POPULATION IS ABOUT 6 MILLION PEOPLE.**

3. The group then compares the two messages.

4. Have the class discuss why messages are changed as they go from person to person. Ask the students what they did if they could not remember part of the message. "Did you just leave it out or substitute something else? Did anyone go back to the previous person if part of the message were forgotten? Did anyone add something to make the story a little more exciting? How do they feel when they can control the message? Does this control give power?"

5. Explain that we play this game everyday at school and home. It is called gossip. "What is gossip? What is rumor?" Ask for a volunteer to read the dictionary definition of the words "gossip," and "rumor." "What happens when you hear statements about others, and then pass them on? Should you pass on messages about others? Does it make a difference if these messages are good or bad news? What happens when you gossip about others—when you pass on news, particularly bad news? Can people get hurt by this? How? Why? Then, why do we gossip? Does gossip give us power?"

6. When the discussion is over, begin the gossip game again, with a very short, encouraging message, such as "I enjoyed talking about this with you today!"

Closure:

"We learned today that messages change when they are repeated over and over again. We learned we can hurt others by telling rumors and repeating gossip. We learned also that people gossip to have power and control, to be the center of what is going on. What we have to decide is which is more important—to be the center of attention or to avoid hurting others. The attention soon goes away, but the hurt to others does not. Nor does the hurt to ourselves when we have told something that is not true. People learn not to trust us. Lack of trust is a huge hurt."

Rosemarie Scotti Hughes, Ph.D. & Pamela C. Kloeppel, Ed.D.

Sailing On:

Have the children select from the library a book about gossip or rumor, and write a book report. Prepare for this in advance with the media specialist.

Have a student read the definition of slander to the class. What is the difference between rumor/gossip/slander?

Have students find five old sayings or proverbs that deal with gossip, such as:

Bad news travels fast.

An ill wind bears no good.

It is an old wives tale.

No news is good news.

Mooring Lines:

Bunting, Anne. *Janet Hamm Needs a Date for the Dance.* Clarion. 1986.

Gilson, Jamie. *4B Goes Wild.* Lothrop, Lee & Shepard. 1983.

Newton, Suzanne. *I Will Call it George's Blues.* Dell. 1986.

It Ain't Necessarily So

Objectives:

Improve oral and writing skills

Understand the concept of stereotyping

Materials:

Dictionary, "??Stereotypes??" handout (page 206).

Procedure:

1. Tell the children that today we are going to examine ideas we have about others to see if those ideas are true or not. For example, we judge people and put them into categories without first finding out anything about the people as individuals. Then we treat these people according to the way we have already categorized them rather than the way they really are.

2. To demonstrate this stereotyping, ask the children to orally finish the sentences below:

    "People with blonde hair are...."

    "I think that everyone who wears glasses is...."

    "People who drive big, new cars are...."

3. This is called stereotyping. Have a student read the definition of stereotyping before proceeding. Discuss its connection to prejudice and bigotry.

4. When children understand the concept, distribute the "??Stereotypes??" handout to each student. Each student is to complete the handout using complete sentences.

5. When all have finished, discuss answers and have children decide if they made judgment statements that are true of all individuals or stereotyped statements. Ask, "Why do we stereotype others? Does it make us feel safer? Have you ever been stereotyped? How did it feel? What happened?"

Closure:

Discuss the importance of seeing a person as an individual. We need to judge others, not by their appearance, but their actions. We need to make friends because of what people do, not on a stereotyped opinion someone holds. Seeing people as individuals and not stereotypes is especially important in our world, where to have peace, all races, colors, creeds, and religions must live together equally.

Sailing On:

Assign the students one of the following:

Creative writing about stereotyping at school by students or teachers

Creative writing about a stereotype held

Creative writing about how they have been treated as a stereotyped group member

Finding and discussing in class examples of magazine ads portraying stereotypes

Finding and discussing in class examples of newspaper stereotyping

Mooring Lines:

Fitzhugh, Louis. *Nobody's Family is Going to Change.* Dell. 1975.

Levoy, Myron. *Alan & Naomi.* Harper & Row. 1977.

Lisle, Janet T. *Afternoon of the Elves.* Orchard. 1989.

Mohr, Nicholasa. *Felita.* Dial. 1979.

Paterson, Katherine. *The Green Gilly Hopkins.* HarperCollins. 1978.

?? STEREOTYPES ??

1. Rich people are _____

2. Fat people are _____

3. Teachers are _____

4. People with dogs are _____

5. Male ballet dancers are _____

6. College students are _____

7. People in wheelchairs are _____

8. Police officers are _____

9. Homeless people are _____

10. Students who fail classes are _____

11. Students who make honor roll are _____

12. Doctors are _____

13. Female truck drivers are _____

14. Gang members are _____

15. Black males are _____

16. Gays are _____

17. People who sell drugs are _____

18. Teenage mothers are _____

19. Grandmothers are _____

20. Only children are _____

21. Native Americans are _____

22. Asians are _____

23. Hispanics are _____

24. Whites are _____

25. Fathers are _____

Rosemarie Scotti Hughes, Ph.D. & Pamela C. Kloeppel, Ed.D.

**Peer Relationships
Fourth Grade Session Six**

Anger, Anxiety, Action

Objectives:

Improve oral and written skills

Understand the concept of conflict resolution through small and large group discussion

Materials:

"Anger, Anxiety, Action" situations (page 208), cut out and put on index cards, "S.A.I.L. Through Conflicts" handout (page 209), pencils and paper.

Procedure:

1. Explain that today we will to learn to handle conflicts with others so we can end these conflicts without fighting. This is called conflict resolution by adults.

2. Divide the class into threes, giving each group a different "Anger, Anxiety, Action" situation.

3. Teach the steps of conflict resolution using the "S.A.I.L. Through Conflicts" handout.

4. Have each group decide on a course of action, following the model. Tell students to assume steps one and two did not work.

5. When all groups are finished, have one student report from each group.

6. At the end of each report, ask the entire class if there are additional actions that could be taken.

7. Repeat until all groups are finished.

Closure:

Now say to the group, "Today we saw how different people would solve various peer problems common to us all. Most groups solved these problems without fighting or getting into trouble. This is the best way to solve problems; this is called conflict resolution." Review the four steps in conflict resolution. (**S.A.I.L.**).

"All too often we handle conflicts by fighting—not by talking to each other. We get angry and we flair out, either with our fists or our mouths. Does fighting really help? It might feel good then but does it help tomorrow? Does it help if we get hurt? If we get suspended? If we hurt others?"

Sailing On:

Ask for volunteers to share a personal conflict situation and then have class determine how it can be solved using S.A.I.L.

Assign creative writing about a current or previous peer conflict and how using the S.A.I.L. method would solve this conflict.

Keep the "S.A.I.L. Through Conflicts" poster in the classroom as a reminder.

Mooring Lines:

Etherington, Frank. *The General.* Annick. 1985.

Greene, Carol. *Robin Hill.* Harper & Row. 1986.

Kurvsa. *The Streets are Free.* Annick. 1985.

Rickman, Ivy. *What's an Average Kid Like Me Doing Way Up Here?* Delacorte. 1983.

Steiner, Barbara. *Oliver Diggs to the Rescue!* Four Winds. 1985.

Anger, Anxiety, Action

The same student cuts in front of you each day in the lunch line; he is bigger than you.	Someone is angry with you and calls your mother a bad name.
The same student asks to borrow a pencil or notebook paper every day, but she never returns it; she is the most popular girl in the class.	Whenever you go to the store the same teenager is there and insists on taking one-half of your money.
The same student blocks you from leaving school each day until you have given him some money. He is a bully and easily wins fights at school.	A classmate constantly teases you because your hand-me-down coat is too big for you and is ripped.
One of your classmates has beaten up your little brother who is in the first grade.	A person you thought was your friend is going to have a birthday party but you are not invited.
You told a personal secret to someone you believed was your friend and who promised not to tell your secret to others-but she did and you are the talk of the town.	A person borrowed your bicycle and broke it; he said it was a cheap bike anyway.

Rosemarie Scotti Hughes, Ph.D. & Pamela C. Kloeppel, Ed.D.

S.A.I.L. Through Conflicts

S. Settle down. Then speak to the person with whom you have a conflict. Be specific in telling how you feel about what is going on. Ask the person to tell his or her feelings, and how you can both settle the conflict. (If this step resolves the conflict, there is no need for other steps.)

A. If the conflict continues, Avoid the person. If this doesn't resolve it, go to the next step.

I. Involve others. Ask adults for help in resolving the problem.

L. Look for alternative solutions.

Ambassadors of Good Will

Objectives:

Improve oral and written skills

Understand that older children are role models for younger children

Materials:

Elementary dictionary; ribbon, cut into 3-inch lengths, one for each child; poster paper and felt tip pen for teacher.

Procedure:

1. Ask who knows the meaning of the word, "ambassador;" let children give their definitions.

2. Have a volunteer read the definition from the dictionary.

3. Explain that an ambassador is a person who represents a government and who speaks for that government. "To represent means to stand for a group of people. For example, if you were in a foreign country and people had never met anyone from _____ (the students' city), those people would form opinions of people from _____ by what they saw and heard you do and say." (If you have students from other countries, you might generate a discussion of what students know about people of that country because of this person.)

4. "In many schools, the fifth grade is the highest grade in the school, so younger students look to fifth grade students to learn ways to behave; fifth graders become role models for younger children; the fifth graders are seen as ambassadors of the school by younger children and the community." (If fifth is not the highest grade in your school, point out that younger children look to older children as role models.)

   "As older students, you send a message to younger students about good behavior in school." Ask, "What do first grade students think if they see you running down the hall?" Use several examples of behavior younger ones would believe appropriate or would try to emulate when they see older students doing it. Include both desirable and undesirable behaviors, e.g.:

   Desirable:

   Picking up litter in the schoolyard

   Being polite in the lunchroom, and so forth.

   Undesirable:

   Writing on bathroom walls

   Dropping paper in the hall, and so forth.

5. To further demonstrate this point, ask the students if they look to middle school students, older siblings, or neighbors as role models. Which of their behaviors do they copy? Which do they not follow? Encourage discussion.

6. Lead the students to the conclusion that they are role models for others, and that they have a great deal of influence in the school.

7. Ask the students to identify positive behaviors they exhibit in school. List these on the board.

8. Have each student state one good behavior he or she will display in school this week. Write the behaviors on poster paper and display this poster as a reminder to carry out the behaviors during the week.

9. Pin a ribbon on each child, explaining that ambassadors have special medals or ribbons; now each student is an official ambassador of the school.

Closure:

Ask the students why being an ambassador might be a difficult job. Make certain they understand that ambassadors must at all times think about how their actions are viewed by others; they must at all times act responsibly, even when they would rather not. "When you are ambassadors for the school, younger children will act as you act; they will do what you do."

Sailing On:

Have the principal pin ribbons on the children to accentuate the "official ambassador status."

Assign a paper, "Monkey See, Monkey Do," in which a student gives examples of copy cat behavior he has observed.

Ask the students to write a short paragraph, poem, or rap, describing how their positive behaviors can influence others.

Written works can be read aloud during the week to reinforce the concept of acting responsibly.

Mooring Lines:

Delton, Judy. *Angel in Charge.* Houghton-Mifflin. 1985.

Ibbitson, John. *The Wimp.* EMC. 1986.

Naylor, Phyllis. *The Agony of Alice.* Atheneum. 1985.

Steiner, Barbara. *Oliver Dibbs and the Dinosaur Case.* Four Winds. 1986.

Inside/Outside

Objectives:

Identify descriptive words through conversation, reading, and writing

Understand that the inner self is often revealed through behavior

Materials:

Drawing paper, crayons and/or markers.

Procedure:

1. Explain that often only close friends and our family know our real inside selves. We often do not trust others enough to reveal our inner selves to them. We are afraid if we do, they will not like us or we will be hurt.

2. Distribute drawing paper and ask the students to fold their drawing paper in half (short side to short side). With the fold on the top, have students draw themselves on the outside section as they believe they appear to others. On the inside, they are to draw something that represents their inner or real selves, i.e., what they are like on the inside. They are to write descriptive words for their inner characteristics, for example, loving, angry, scared, eager. (You may want to generate some words first from the class to help students in identification.)

3. When students are finished, ask if their inside drawings are different from their outside drawings. Invite students to discuss their drawings telling how they are different inside and outside. Can they give the reason for the difference? Allow students the freedom to "pass" if they are not comfortable in the discussion.

4. Ask the students to brainstorm ways that class members can get to know each other's inside selves a little better, and how to show "inside" qualities since they can't be visibly seen by others.

5. Discuss the benefits of letting others know more about ourselves and learning more about others (i.e., understanding, cooperation).

Closure:

End the discussion by explaining the importance of accepting each other as we are, "We may not always like everyone equally well, in fact, there may be people we don't like at all. But if people are not hurting us or others they have a right to be as they are and we have the responsibility to accept them as they are—to let them be their real selves. Also, we have the right to be our real selves." End by reading this poem from Lalle's, *At Least I'm Getting Better*, 506 Independence Drive, Harleysville, PA 19438:

We're O.K.

I like me and
I like you,
Together there's a lot that
We can do.

We're not the same
In every way,
But I'm O.K. and
You're O.K.

Rosemarie Scotti Hughes, Ph.D. & Pamela C. Kloeppel, Ed.D.

Sailing On:

Ask the students to read a biography or autobiography and write a book report on the character's inner qualities and how these qualities are revealed.

This can be an appropriate time for the teacher to self-disclose, comparing your inside and outside self. Sharing yourself might encourage others to share (e.g., hobbies you may have of which children are unaware, a happy event in your life, a time when you may have felt afraid).

Have students discuss famous literary characters or real people whose inside qualities are shown by their lives and work. Some examples are listed below:

Jesse Jackson	dedicated to civil rights, ambitious
Arthur Ash	compassionate, moral, private
Maya Angelou	persistence, understanding, literary talent
Michael Jordan	hard worker, talented
Sally Ride	patriot, loyal
Mike Tyson	hot headed, cocky
Mother Theresa	dedicated to sick and poor, peace loving
Abraham Lincoln	belief in freedom, dedicated to the country
Aldolph Hitler	evil, greedy, ambitious, power hungry

The list of famous people identified can support current instructional goals, e.g., famous scientists, explorers, leaders, presidents, authors, artists, and so forth.

Mooring Lines:

Baven, Marion. *Like Mother, Like Daughter*. Houghton-Mifflin. 1985.
Carrick, Carol. *Stay Away from Simon*. Clarion. 1985.
Colman, Hilda. *Nobody Told Me What I Needed to Know*. Morrow. 1984.
Hines, Anna. *Cossie Bowen Takes Witch Lessons*. E.P. Dutton. 1985.
Silverstein, Shel. *The Giving Tree*. HarperCollins. 1964.

How Do Others See Me?

Objectives:

Improve expressive skills, both oral and written

Understand the circular relationship of behavior and perception

Materials:

Elementary dictionary, "Perception of/Treatment Toward" handout, page 216), index cards and pencils.

Procedure:

1. Ask the children if anyone has ever heard his or her own voice on a tape recorder? Have the children explain what this was like. What did they think about the sound of their own voice? Explain that all of us sound different to ourselves than we do to others. We are hearing ourselves from the inside; others hear us from the outside with the interference of the environment and their own hearing "equipment."

2. "When we see ourselves in a photograph, we often say, 'That doesn't look like me!' That's because we have a certain mental picture of ourselves and this may be different from what the camera records." Ask the students to share examples in their experience.

3. "It is the same with our behavior. Others often see qualities of which we are not aware, or which we think we are hiding. You may say 'please' and 'thank you' because it is routine to you, and others see you as considerate. You may not think of yourself as considerate and would be pleased to be thought of in that manner. When you don't use these words you may be seen as inconsiderate, when you are not. People may have perceptions of us that are different from our own."

5. Have a volunteer read the definition of perception from the dictionary. Have students discuss accurate and inaccurate perceptions they have had of people.

6. Have the students sit in a circle and distribute index cards; ask them to write their names and one quality that they have on the card. Collect cards. Have each child take a turn sitting in the center of the circle with others telling one positive thing about this person. As the positives are given write down these qualities on the child's index card.

7. When all have had their turn, return the cards, and ask the children to compare what they wrote with what others said about them.

8. Discuss whether perceptions of others were the same or different from self-perception. "Were some of you surprised by what the others said? Did you agree or disagree with what was said? Why? Were there some qualities you thought you had that were not mentioned? How can you help people know about these qualities?"

Rosemarie Scotti Hughes, Ph.D. & Pamela C. Kloeppel, Ed.D.

Closure:

"Many times people's perception of us is just what we want it to be; other times it is not. Why? As we learned today others' perception of us is the result of our behavior. The perception others have of us influences the way they act toward us. Sometimes our own behaviors don't show our positive qualities, and people do not treat us as we would like. Therefore, we control the way others treat us—by the way we act. So if we don't like how we are treated by others, we can change this treatment, by changing our behavior."

Sailing On:

Assign a creative writing paper about a personal behavior liked or disliked. Students are to explain why, and either how the liked behavior can continue to be used or how the disliked behavior can be changed.

If time allows give each student a turn speaking and listening to his own voice on a tape recorder.

Instead of, or in addition to, #6 and #7, have students complete and discuss, "Perception of/Treatment Toward" handout.

Mooring Lines:

Byars, Betsy Caromer. *The Animal, the Vegetable, and John D. Jones*. Dell. 1983.

Mauser, Pat Rhoads. *A Bundle of Sticks*. Atheneum. 1987.

Perl, Lela. *The Telltale Summer of Tina C*. Scholastic. 1984.

Perception of/Treatment Toward

Listed below are some of the perceptions we have of other people; next to each perception list the way you might treat that person.

bully _____

flirt _____

tattle tale _____

helpful _____

teacher's pet _____

kind _____

greedy _____

bossy _____

whiner _____

nice _____

popular _____

risk taker _____

loud _____

rude _____

considerate _____

trustworthy _____

know-it-all _____

dumb _____

smart _____

clown _____

sloppy _____

angry _____

violent _____

happy _____

Rosemarie Scotti Hughes, Ph.D. & Pamela C. Kloeppel, Ed.D.

Peer Relationships
Fifth Grade Session Four

Curtain Going Up

Objectives:

Dramatize and read about conflict resolution behaviors

Practice conflict resolution

Materials:

"Teasing Bullying Scenarios" (page 218), "Who is Really Winning?" handout (page 218).

Procedure:

1. Ask the children how they feel when someone teases or bullies them. Encourage them to give specific examples of being teased or bullied and how it felt. Discuss what they did when teased. Are they still being teased?

2. Ask how they feel when someone bullies them; again, ask for specific examples. Then, discuss what they do when bullied. Ask, "Do teasing and bullying sometimes go together?" Again, have the students discuss, using specific examples and sharing feelings. Ask them how they handle such situations.

3. Ask what the students would like to do when they are teased or bullied. Some may indicate a preference for fighting back; discuss the possible consequences of that.

4. Ask the students if they are satisfied with their own actions when they are bullied or teased? "Do you get mad at yourself later because you let someone get to you? Do you think later of something you should have said or done?"

5. Explain, "Today we are going to practice appropriate responses to being bullied and teased so we will know what to do in the future—so we will feel better about ourselves." Have a student read "Who is Really Winning" handout and post it in the rooms.

6. Role play each scenario on the next page. After each role play discuss how the person bullied or teased feels, and what can they do? Can they handle it alone? Do they need adult help? Are they being a narc or tattle-tale by asking for adult help?

Closure:

At the end of all role plays ask the students to state one useful thing they learned from today's session.

Mooring Lines:

Conford, Ellen. *The Revenge of the Incredible Dr. Rancid and His Youthful Assistant.* Jeffrey, Little, Brown. 1980.

Mauser, Pat Rhoads. *A Bundle of Sticks.* Atheneum. 1987.

Wartski, Maureen Crane. *A Long Way from Home.* New America Library. 1982.

Teasing/Bullying Scenarios

1. Bill is walking home from school when some girls, walking behind him, start chanting, "Billy loves Amanda, Billy loves Amanda." They giggle and laugh, and one says, very loudly, that she heard Billy kissed Amanda before school. They start chanting again.

2. David is tall and thin. He's rather clumsy and not good at sports; and he goes to some special classes. He wears glasses and has a hearing aid in one ear. In PE, they are playing basketball. When it is David's turn to shoot, some of the students start making jeering noises and saying, "OK, String Bean, use those four eyes and try to make a shot." Someone else says, "No sense to yell at him; he can't hear you anyway" and laughs. David misses all the shots he tries. When the group is walking back to class, someone behind him whispers, "Dumb David, dumb David."

3. Mary walks to school. Every Monday she brings money to buy lunch for the week. Last Monday, some bigger girls stopped her before school and demanded her money. They told Mary that if she told anyone about this, they would beat her up. Mary went without lunch all week. The next Monday, the same thing happened.

4. Every day walking home from school, a middle school student grabs Sandra's arm and twists it until Sandra begs him to stop. Then he calls her a name that makes her feel worse.

Who is Really Winning?

If someone calls you a name

They want you to get angry.

If you get angry

Who is really winning?

If someone teases you

They want you to get upset.

If you get upset

Who is really winning?

So before you act... THINK,

"Who do I really want to win?"

Rosemarie Scotti Hughes, Ph.D. & Pamela C. Kloeppel, Ed.D.

Peer Relationships
Fifth Grade Session Five

Stories to Live By

Objectives:

Improve reading and writing skills

Identify desirable role models in real or fictional characters

Materials:

Writing paper and pencils, blackboard and chalk, or chartpaper and marker.

Procedure:

1. Assign the students a book to read. Books can be either fact or fiction, and should depict a variety of characters. Some characters would make good friends; some would not. Make a list in advance with the help of the media specialist.

2. After reading their book, the students are to list the qualities of one character and put a checkmark next to the qualities that would make this character a good friend.

3. They are then to write a paragraph about this character. They should use the structure of (character) _____ of (book title) _____ would make a good friend because _____ .

4. Have the children bring their paragraphs to class and read them aloud. Before reading, they are to write the character's name on the board. Ask each reader whether he or she would like to be like the character. Why? If the response is positive ask the student one way he or she can imitate the qualities of this character at school. If the response is negative, ask which quality of the character should be changed and why.

5. Remind the students of the day when they wore ribbons and were Ambassadors of Good Will in school. Which of their story characters would be Ambassadors of Good Will? Circle those names on the board.

Closure:

"We have discussed many literary characters today; some were fictional, some were real. Some would make good friends; some would not. No matter when or where our characters lived, the same qualities made them either good friends or poor friends. People are good friends who care for others, treat others with kindness and respect, keep their confidences, and remain loyal. Poor friends are the opposite—they think first of their own wants, are mean or kind depending on what they have to gain, tell confidences for power or status, and are loyal only to themselves. What kind of friend will people say and write that you are?" Ask the students to answer this question to themselves.

Sailing On:

Ask each child, in a follow-up session, to identify one story character and state one of the character's qualities he will agree to imitate in school the next day. An example might be Abraham Lincoln with a statement to be fair and treat others equally, or Casper the Friendly Ghost, with a statement to be a friend to all.

Mooring Lines:

Corcoran, Barbara. *Child of the Morning.* American Printing House for the Blind. 1982.

Cuyler, Margery S. *The Trouble with Soap.* Dutton Children's. 1982.

DeClements, Barthe. *Nothing's Fair in Fifth Grade.* Viking Penguin. 1981.

Fox, Paula. *Portrait of Ivan.* Bradbury. 1969.

Hughes, Dean. *Switching Tracks.* Atheneum. 1982.

Gurwitz, Johanna. *The Law of Gravity.* William Morrow. 1978.

Gurwitz, Johanna. *Tough-Luck Karen.* William Morrow. 1982.

Kent, Deborah. *Belonging: A Novel.* Putnam Berkley. 1979.

Peer Relationships
Fifth Grade Session Six
Communication's the Key

Objectives:

Role play

Practice conflict resolution skills

Materials:

"Conflict Consequences" sheet (page 223).

Procedure:

1. "We learned earlier the S.A.I.L. method of handling conflicts with others:

   S Settle down and speak to the other person.

   A Avoid the person/situation.

   I Involve others.

   L Look for other solutions.

   When you have a conflict with another, the first step is to speak to the person who is bothering you. How you speak to the other person and what you say is very important. There are certain dos and don'ts (write these on the board) of communication when we are angry.

   Do:

   Talk to the person in private.

   Say what he or she did that you did not like.

   Tell the person how you feel about what he or she did.

   Explain what you want the person to change.

   Don't:

   Talk about past hurts/problems.

   Use put downs.

   Make threats.

   Tell other people about it, until you have talked to the person first."

2. "Today we are going to practice these steps/rules of conflict resolution." Ask for two or three students to role play each situation on the "Conflict Consequences" worksheet.

3. After each role play ask the actors to discuss their feelings. Ask if they acted differently in the role play, using these "dos and don'ts" than they would have acted normally. Would this work for them in real life? Why? Why not?

4. Ask for feedback from the other students. Were all the dos and don'ts followed? Did they follow the steps? Would this work for them in real life? Why? Why not?

Closure:

"Sometimes people make us angry and try to hurt us. Often, but not always, we can stop this person from hurting us now and in the future by using the "dos and don'ts" of communication. Sharing feelings and telling the person exactly what is bothering you often helps—especially, when you talk in private. In private, no one has to put on a show for others. No one has to save face. No one has to play the big shot. Sometimes, however, no amount of talking helps. Sometimes avoiding the person will do the trick. But sometimes you have to seek help from others, from me, your teacher, the counselor, the principal, your parents, the police. We are all here for you. Remember to think first, then act whenever you are angry or hurt."

Sailing On:

Ask the students to record incidents that happen to them this week and how they use the "dos and don'ts" of resolving conflicts in each situation. These writings are to be kept in a "Conflict Resolution" journal for one month. Allow daily writing time in class. Hold weekly discussions of sharing resolutions of conflict.

Mooring Lines:

Golding, William. *Lord of the Flies*. Coward-McCann. 1962.

Knudson, R. Rozanne. *Zanbanger*. HarperCollins. 1977.

Platt, Kin. *The Ape Inside Me*. HarperCollins. 1979.

Rosemarie Scotti Hughes, Ph.D. & Pamela C. Kloeppel, Ed.D.

Conflict Consequences

You are spending the night with a friend. After everyone else in the family is asleep your friend suggests you try some of his or her mom's alcohol. You refuse. The next day, everyone in class is calling you a sissy. What would you say?

You and your friend are at the park. Two older boys come over and offer you some drugs. Your friend says yes. You leave. What would you say at the park? What would you say later to your friend.

At school your classmate suggests the two of you stop up the commode with toilet tissue. Your friend says, "We won't get caught, scaredy cat." You refuse and leave, but your classmate gets caught. He blames you for telling. You didn't tell. What would you say?

A new boy just moved down the street and he is bigger than you. He likes your bike; he has an old bicycle. One day he grabs the bike from you and rides it to the store. What would you say?

You want to go play with a friend, but your mother insists you go to the grocery store for her. You stop on the way to visit your friend and are late getting home. Your mom is angry. What would you say?

Your best friend's father is out-of-town, but he left his keys in the car. Your friend, who is a fifth grader like you , wants to take you for a ride. You won't go. Now everyone knows you refused to have any fun. What would you say?

Two kids in class have been teasing you for doing your homework instead of playing with them after school. They are saying you are stuck up and think you are better than they are. What would you say?

One student always asks you for money. He is bigger than you and you are frightened of him. What would you say?

Sally wants you to cut school one day to go to the beach. She has asked you over and over again and now is calling you a chicken. What would you say?

Johnny often borrows your cassette player; now he has finally broken it and he doesn't plan on replacing it. What would you say?

The same person always pushes ahead of you in the lunch line. He says you are fat and don't need to eat. What would you say?

Notes:

Rosemarie Scotti Hughes, Ph.D. & Pamela C. Kloeppel, Ed.D.